"Andrew Farley is one of the best young writers yet most mature thinkers in the church today. Read *God without Religion* to hear the voice of a twenty-first-century Bonhoeffer who shows how to ring in the good times when Jesus (not religion) is the *cantus firmus*, the enduring melody, of our lives." —**Leonard Sweet**, bestselling author; professor, Drew University and George Fox University

"Never have I encountered a book that so clearly and biblically explains new covenant Christianity. If you want to dump the religious burden and live in the true freedom and joy of Christ, *God without Religion* is for you." —**David Gregory**, bestselling author of *Dinner with a Perfect Stranger* and *The Rest of the Gospel*

"*God without Religion* is brave, genius, and full of the best kind of hope. Andrew Farley offers us a clear, more joy-filled, and peaceful route to God, without religion! And we need that now more than ever." —**Matthew Paul Turner**, bestselling author of *Churched* and *Hear No Evil*

"This is a book that every Christian simply must read before going one more step in their walk with Christ. Don't waste another day living under religious bondage. Stop everything you're doing and read this book now." —**Darin Hufford**, bestselling author of *The Misunderstood God*

"Andrew Farley exquisitely communicates the beauty of grace. He shows us how to live every moment of every day from the intimate relationship with Christ that is ours to enjoy. If you want to soak in the abundance of God's love, I highly recommend *God without Religion*." —**Jan Mugele**, twenty-year Wycliffe missionary to the Chinantec people in Oaxaca, Mexico

"Get ready for a life-changing adventure. A master storyteller, Farley turns conventional thinking on its ear with this paradigm-shifting *tour de force*. If you read one Christian book this year, let this be it!" —**John McCuin**, professor, Dallas Baptist University

"Is it really possible to enjoy intimacy with God without the trappings of religious expectation, guilt, and shame? If it sounds too good to be true, you'll be blown away by this book! Farley leads us out of religiosity and into the exhilarating reality of knowing Jesus as *life*." —**Bob Perdue**, lead pastor, Grace Life Community Church, Bristow, VA

"Andrew Farley stands with the most insightful and engaging Christian authors of our time. God has equipped this man with an extraordinary ability to grasp and illuminate Scripture with vivid clarity. *God without Religion* may be the most Christ-centered book you'll ever read." —**Chip Polk**, cofounder, Ragtown Gospel Theater, Post, TX

"The message of *God without Religion* is theologically rich, profoundly simple, and deeply life changing. This is exactly what you'd expect from an author who doesn't just talk about God's grace but has experienced it firsthand." —**Jeremy White**, lead pastor, Valley Church, Vacaville, CA

"Andrew Farley introduces us to a Father who is more interested in us resting in him than working for him. With so many Christians trying hard to measure up, *God without Religion* is timely and relevant. Read this book to discover the 'Like' button on your heart and the God who has clicked it." —**Andy Knight**, executive director of Lifetime Guarantee; designer for LifeChurch.tv

"In *God without Religion*, Andrew Farley returns with inspired clarity to make the solid biblical case that freedom is what God has always intended for us. The presentation of these truths just doesn't get any better. I will forever be thankful for the hope presented in this book." —**Danny Gutierrez**, pastor and missionary, Bloom Church, Minneapolis, MN

GOD

~~RELIGION~~ WITHOUT

GOD

WITHOUT ~~RELIGION~~

CAN IT REALLY BE THIS SIMPLE?

ANDREW FARLEY

BakerBooks

a division of Baker Publishing Group

Grand Rapids, MI

Published by Baker Books
a division of Baker Publishing Group
P.O. Box 6287, Grand Rapids, MI 49516-6287
www.bakerbooks.com

Paperback edition published 2011
ISBN 978-0-8010-1487-1

Printed in the United States of America

The Library of Congress has cataloged the original edition of this book as follows:
Farley, Andrew, 1972–
    God without religion : can it really be this simple? / Andrew Farley.
      p. cm.
    ISBN 978-0-8010-1399-7 (cloth)
    1. Christian Life. I. Title
    BV4501.3.F357 2011
    248.4—dc22   2010049698

Published in association with the literary agency of Alive Communications, Inc., 7680 Goddard Street, Suite 200, Colorado Springs, CO 80920, www.alivecommunications.com.

14   15   16   17   7 6 5 4 3

For my son, Gavin.
How much joy it brings me just to watch you play!

CONTENTS

re-li-gion \ri-ˈli-jən\ (noun)

A return to bondage. The word *religion* is traced to the Latin *re* meaning "again" and *ligare* meaning "to bind."

THE EXTORTIONIST

Drew Dog! How you doin', Drew Dog? Hey, listen, I know what happened to your stuff, and I can get it back for you. Crime Stoppers offers a thousand dollars for information about a burglary. But if you give me a thousand bucks, I'll get your stuff back right away."

We'd been robbed. While our family was away, our Indiana home had been cleaned out. Now, just one week later, this guy was on our doorstep trying to extort money. On top of that, I knew him! He had come by a month ago asking to rake leaves in our yard, and we hired him. Apparently, he'd taken that opportunity to scope out our place and strategize his entry through a rear window.

Welcome to life in downtown South Bend. We'd only been living there a few months. This was the latest in a series of indicators that maybe there was a *reason* our home had been so affordable.

"Hang on just a minute," I told the guy. "I've got something I need to take care of in the kitchen. I'll be right back." I closed the door and headed to the kitchen to call the police. When I returned, I expected the guy to be gone.

He was still there.

I kept him talking. We chatted about, you know, the weather and sports. After several minutes, the police pulled up and hauled him away for questioning. We were sure we'd never see him again.

Knock. Knock.

It had only been a couple of hours. I peered out the window to see who was on the front porch. Sure enough, it was him. I opened the door to a loud shout. "Drew Dog, I went downtown for you! I got knocked around for you! You owe me, Drew Dog! You owe me!"

In a weird way, I enjoyed the nickname. But I wasn't sure how to respond, so I fell back on what had worked in the past. "Hang on just a minute. I've got something in the kitchen I need to take care of. I'll be right back," I said.

This time I expected him to catch on. But upon my return from the kitchen, he was, yet again, still there. It was just a few minutes of chitchat before the squad car pulled up. Once again, they hauled him away. Surely this time they'd pin something on him—harassment, or disturbing the peace, or something.

Knock. Knock. Knock.

It was now close to midnight. I crept downstairs and looked out the window. Yeah, it was him. What was with this guy? Wasn't he getting the message? I opened the door for the third time that night.

"Drew Dog, I'm cold. I'm homeless. I need some gloves."

I held up my hand to signal that I needed just a minute to check on something. By now *you* know the drill, but did he? I headed to the kitchen and told the police he was back for the third time. Then I returned to the front door. There he was, waiting patiently for me.

Remembering our previous small talk, I said, "Homeless? I thought you said you live at 211 West Young Street, Apartment B."

Feeling caught in his lie, he said, "Oh yeah, well, I'm cold. You got any gloves?"

I looked around the front hall. A pair of my wife's furry pink gloves was right there. My wife would've preferred that I continue the search, but I handed him the lovely gloves and said, "Here you go. Now, the best thing to do is just leave."

"Okay," he said, "but can I jump your fence?"

"Jump our fence? No, just walk around, man," I said.

"C'mon, Drew Dog, I always jump the fence when I go through your yard!" he said.

His reply wasn't exactly comforting. After that night, we began looking for ways to move! "Look, man, you gotta get out of here. The police are on their way again," I said.

He seemed surprised. But he took my word for it and headed off down the street. When the police pulled up, I pointed in his direction, and they set off in pursuit.

That was the last we saw of him for a while. But then one beautiful fall afternoon the following year . . .

Knock. Knock.

I opened the door and was greeted with, "Drew Dog! How you doin', Drew Dog? Listen, you got any work for me? Maybe I could rake your leaves again?"

"Just a minute," I said. "I've got something in the kitchen I need to take care of."

RELIGIOUS ROBBERY

After the burglary, we felt pretty insecure. Every night we closed the curtains up tight, and every noise made us jump. Before long, we purchased an expensive alarm system, installing motion sensors on our windows and throughout the house. The burglars had taken $13,000 in belongings, but our sense of security was the most valuable thing they stole.

In much the same way, we can fall victim to spiritual burglary. *Religion* is a thief that's delighted to clean us out. Religion plots to rob us of our spiritual possessions and our sense of security. Oh, and religion is happy to drop by our doorstep later to offer it all back.

At a price.

So how can we keep our confident rest in Jesus from being stolen and held for ransom? *By abandoning any form of religion.*

Religion plots to rob us and offer it all back at a price.

Is it safe to just abandon religion? As we'll see, it's not only safe; it's God's passionate desire for us. But if we're to escape the clutches of religion, we need to see religion for what it truly is. And we need to be certain there's another way.

As I shared the true story of our experience with burglary and extortion, you probably wondered, "Why did he keep opening the door?"

Good question.

In hindsight, I realize I shouldn't have. It would've been safer to ignore the burglar and his offer. I guess I thought there might be some way to get our stuff back. Similarly, the trouble with religion is that it appeals to our human appetites. When we've lost a sense of belonging in God's kingdom or the feeling of closeness to the King, we may look to religion for answers. It's difficult to simply ignore religion, shutting the door on its offers. And we can't afford to ignore religion unless we're *certain* we already have everything we need to make life work, apart from religion.

This book is an invitation to consider the idea that we Christians need no religion of any sort. That instead we already have everything we need to experience an intimate relationship with Jesus. Maybe our only real trouble is that we just don't know what we have.

PART 1

MENNONITE MOTORBOAT

[The law] is a widower in search
of a girlfriend, and he has no
problem finding one at church.

Juan Carlos Ortiz (1961–)

1

I wrote my first book, *The Naked Gospel*, on a Sony laptop. It began crashing pretty often during the last couple of months of finishing the book. So after I finished the book, I decided I'd shop for a new laptop.

Now I'm typing away on my new Apple MacBook. Yeah, I switched teams. But for you die-hard PC fans, let me explain what happened to me.

I had done my research ahead of time. I was well aware that *Consumer Reports* rated MacBooks as the most reliable. I also knew that Apple had top-rated customer service. But that's not what got me.

There I was, standing in front of *so many* PC-compatible laptops in my price range. And there was only one model from Apple. I had never owned a MacBook, and the learning curve with a new operating system seemed unnecessary. But just as I was ready to walk away with another PC, it happened. One sly comment from the savvy salesperson, and I was sold.

"You know, nowadays you can install Windows software on a MacBook. You can use the older, familiar operating system on your new Mac hardware."

Next thing I knew, I was at the checkout with MacBook in hand. The *compatibility* of the old and familiar with the new and shiny was precisely what convinced me.

Which notebook computer was the most reliable? The MacBook. And which had the best customer service? The MacBook. Still, what I wanted was a *compromise* so the transition would seem easier. I wasn't comfortable with making a radical change, at least not without "training wheels."

It's not much different when it comes to the old way of religion and the new way God longs for us to know. We're used to thinking we need religion to keep us on the straight and narrow. Even when we buy into the simplicity of "Jesus plus nothing" for salvation, we might try to make Jesus fit *alongside* some religion for the long haul. Just like I was tempted to do with the MacBook, we end up mixing the old with the new.

God's simple message for us is like our New Year's declaration "Out with the old and in with the new." Through the voices of New Testament writers, God pleads with us to firmly place our confidence in his new way, not allowing even a hint of religion to creep in. God wants us to put all our stock in one place, but that feels risky. To be safe, we'd rather take our religion along for the ride.

By the way, I never ended up downloading any PC software onto my MacBook. When I got home, everything just worked. It was incredibly easy to use. I guess I forgot all about the old operating system once I realized Apple's new way was simpler and better.

How do you completely drop the old way of religion? Easy. Just get to know God's new way. Then there's no looking back.

INCOMPATIBLE JESUS

Even if we want to mix old-time religion with our new-found life in Christ, we really can't. At least, not if we want to keep Jesus in the picture. Yeah, you can put PC programs on a MacBook, but you can't make Jesus fit with the old way of the law.

Here's one reason why: the *lineage* of Jesus.

The lineage of Jesus? Yes, Jesus's lineage is one of the strongest arguments for abandoning the old way and grabbing on exclusively to a brand-new way.

Today, we call upon Jesus as our high priest, our representative before God. But Jesus was born into the tribe of Judah. And here's what Moses, author of the law, said about priests serving from the tribe of Judah: Nothing. Zero. Zilch. Moses never once mentioned any priest being allowed to come from the tribe of Judah. God himself forbade such an idea. God told Moses that *only* the tribe of Levi was to serve as priests:

> You can't make Jesus fit with the old way of the law.

> [Jesus] belonged to a different tribe, and no one from that tribe has ever served at the altar. For it is clear that our Lord descended from Judah, and *in regard to that tribe Moses said nothing about priests.* (Heb. 7:13–14)

For thousands of years, Old Testament priests came from only one place—the tribe of Levi. Then Jesus shows up on the scene, breaking all the rules. He's an illegal priest with a "passport" that disqualifies him for priesthood.

Why would God do this? Why would he arrange for Jesus to be born into the tribe of Judah? It would've been a lot easier sell if Jesus had been from the tribe of Levi. The Jews would've recognized his Levitical authority. They could've just tweaked their understanding of Moses to make room for what Jesus was adding to the mix.

Apparently, God wasn't looking for a smooth transition. He wanted to turn everything upside down. And he began by having Jesus be an *unqualified* priest according to the law.

NEW PRIEST = NEW WAY

We look to Jesus as our representative before God. But how can Jesus legitimately be our priest if the law won't allow it? The answer is simple, and it comes straight from Scripture:

> For when there is a *change of the priesthood* there must also be a *change of the law*. (Heb. 7:12)

Because there's a new kind of priest in town, God is telling us we can't mix in the old way of the law. To do so involves a serious contradiction.

Do you see it? Against the backdrop of thousands of years of doing things one way, God has now done it another way. Former priests came from Levi, but now no more. Since our priest has a different lineage, the old way is entirely incompatible with him. When there's a change of priesthood, the *whole* system must change.

There's more. The writer of Hebrews says Jesus "was designated by God to be high priest in the order of Melchizedek" (Heb. 5:10). You can just see the Jewish readers going, "Melchizedek, Melchizedek . . . boy, that name sounds familiar." They thumb through the Old Testament and find one reference to him as "king of Salem" (Gen. 14:18). And Hebrews describes him as "without genealogy" (Heb. 7:3). Apparently, Mel had no known father or mother. He came out of nowhere! But Abraham respected Mel as having a unique priesthood from God. And this was *more than four hundred years before the law.*

> When there's a change of priesthood, the *whole* system must change.

So let's get this straight. According to the law, Jesus is from the wrong tribe to be a priest? He has the wrong lineage? On top of that, his priesthood is in the order of Melchizedek, a mystery man who lived *before* the law? Yes, that's right. And for these reasons, the old way of the law and Jesus just don't mix.

Our heavenly high priest invites us to a whole new way.

2

ew way, old way—doesn't make much difference! If you knew me, you'd understand. I'm just not that good at religion. I'm not that committed. I'm a weak Christian by any measure."

Maybe you think you've committed some pretty big sins. Or maybe you still have some major struggles going on. So you think the idea of enjoying God to the fullest can't possibly apply to you. If so, I'd like to ask you a question:

How many people have you killed?

Yes, you read that one right. How many people have you killed? I ask you this question, because much of the Bible was written by murderers. Moses killed an Egyptian in rage. David killed a guy to steal his wife. And Paul killed Christians in religious pride. Here's a sample of Paul's ugly resume:

> I put many of the saints in prison, and when they were *put to death, I cast my vote against them.* Many a time I went from one synagogue to another *to have them punished,*

and I tried to force them to blaspheme. In my obsession against them, I even went to foreign cities *to persecute them*. (Acts 26:10–11)

In comparison with killing Christians, how big are *your* sins? And just how "different" is your situation? Let's face it—the only thing that stops us from enjoying God is *not believing we are qualified*. But here's a news flash for you: Your sins are small. Your God is big. And you are qualified.

OUR CONTRACT WITH GOD

So how can we experience God without religion? The key, I believe, is in understanding our contract with God.

Contract? Yes, contract. Our contract with God is better than we can possibly imagine. It's better than the double-minded religion we've concocted. It's better than the Christian jargon we've fabricated. And it's better than the old way we've been peddling alongside Jesus ever since the early church.

Your sins are small. Your God is big. And you are qualified.

Our contract with God invites us to experience something Old Testament people only dreamed of. Apparently, they never enjoyed what we have now. The heroes of the Old Testament were more dedicated than nearly any of us today. But that doesn't seem to matter. We still get a better deal than they had:

These were all commended for their faith, yet *none of them received* what had been promised. God had planned

something better for us so that only together with us would
they be made perfect. (Heb. 11:39–40)

Why is our contract with God so much better these days?
To answer that one, let's start with a marriage on the rocks.

A GOD OF DIVORCE?

David and Shelly had been married for nine years. For the
first few years, it was like heaven. But little did David know
that Shelly had plans for him to change, or else.

Shelly really liked David but saw things in him that she
planned to "work on." If she could change him, she'd stick
with him. But if David didn't change, well, that would leave
the door open to who knows what—maybe even divorce.

David entered the marriage a bit naïve. He assumed
Shelly was in it for life. Boy, was he surprised when Shelly
began to complain about his lazy habits, his low-paying
job, and his lack of drive. "Why can't you be more like
your brother? He has a plan and a future. He knows where
he's going in life. You don't have a clue! Do you expect me
to stick around if you stay in the same dead-end job and
don't get us out of this hole?"

David was a hard worker. He worked two jobs: con-
struction during the week and car sales on Saturdays. He
was doing *everything* he could. But it wasn't good enough
for Shelly. Her standards were just too high. At least once
every few months, she'd really go after him. She'd tear him
down and make him feel like nothing. Then she'd threaten
to leave him. David would apologize and make frantic attempts to please her.

David worked double shifts. Then he changed jobs to make more money. Still Shelly complained that David wasn't giving her the life that she'd hoped for.

David's heart was broken. He was absolutely in love with Shelly and wanted nothing more than to please her. He just lacked the ability to do it! No matter how hard he tried, he couldn't keep her happy.

> God's marriage contract with us truly means "in sickness and in health."

Eventually, Shelly made her decision. She met with a lawyer and issued David the papers. It would soon be over, and she could find someone capable of giving her what David could not.

Sound like a marriage you'd enjoy? How'd you like to be David? Most of us would take a pass on that one! But isn't this exactly what it'd be like for us if we could *lose our salvation*? We'd be married (spiritually) to a spouse who was constantly evaluating us and ready to drop the hammer of divorce.

God hates divorce. We know this from Scripture. Yet those who claim we can lose our salvation are saying we become the bride of Christ, but God will divorce us if we don't perform to his standards!

A WHOLE NEW WAY

As we call upon Jesus, we enter into a new way of relating to God. This new way eliminates even the remote possibility of God "divorcing" us. God's marriage contract with us truly means "in sickness and in health." Jesus introduced a better contract with God (Heb. 7:22; 9:15). It's unlike anything before. It enables us to enjoy God without the rocky road of religion. Here's what it's all about:

> Heads up! The days are coming
>> when I'll set up a new plan
>> for dealing with Israel and Judah.
> I'll throw out the old plan
>> I set up with their ancestors
>> when I led them by the hand out of Egypt.
> *They didn't keep their part of the bargain,*
>> *so I looked away* and let it go.
> This new plan I'm making with Israel
>> isn't going to be written on paper,
>> isn't going to be chiseled in stone;
> This time I'm writing out the plan *in* them,
>> carving it *on the lining of their hearts.*
> I'll be their God,
>> they'll be my people.
> They won't go to school to learn about me,
>> or buy a book called *God in Five Easy Lessons.*
> *They'll all get to know me* firsthand,
>> the little and the big, the small and the great.
> They'll get to know me by being kindly forgiven,
>> with *the slate of their sins forever wiped clean.*
>> (Heb. 8:8–12 Message)

Did you notice the trouble with the old way of religion? Just like David's failure to meet Shelly's expectations, it says Israel "didn't keep their part of the bargain" (v. 9 Message). And the result? God looked away from them.

But under this new contract, that problem is *solved.*

First, God stamps his desires on our hearts, so that we will want what he wants. Second, we receive a place at the table, as part of God's family. "They'll all get to know me firsthand," he says, "by being kindly forgiven, with the slate of their sins forever wiped clean" (vv. 11–12 Message). A brand-new heart and a clean slate make God's new way radically different.

Everyone under the old way "did not remain faithful to my covenant, and I turned away from them" (Heb. 8:9). In the Old Testament, even the most dedicated religious servants failed to impress God and stay in his good graces. That's a problem, since most of us today won't exert the same efforts! Old Testament servants worked tirelessly to get it all right. And God still turned away from them. It just wasn't good enough.

But God said, "I'll throw out the old plan" (Heb. 8:9 Message). And this new way came on the scene to solve everything. The secret to this new way is this: *it's not about us*. Instead, it's about God's faithfulness *to himself*!

It's Not about You!

God's new contract is very different. Our performance is not in focus. We're not the ones signing the contract. Sure, we benefit from it. But we don't enact it or sustain it. The old problem of faithfulness is cured by God's new solution. Now it's about someone else's faithfulness.

Under the old way, "God found fault with the people" (Heb. 8:8). Under the new way, God made *a promise to himself*. He didn't want to involve anyone else who might waver or change. He'd already been down that road!

God did this so that, *by two unchangeable things* in which *it is impossible for God to lie*, we who have fled to take hold of the hope offered to us may be greatly encouraged. We have this hope as *an anchor for the soul*, firm and secure. (Heb. 6:18–19)

What are the two unchangeable things? God and God. We're not involved in the bargain, because God knew how that would turn out! Instead, this new contract is about God's promise to himself. God's no liar. That's why his new plan is "an anchor for the soul, *firm* and *secure*" (Heb. 6:19).

Picture the mythological Greek character Atlas, carrying the world on his shoulders. This reminds me of Christians who are overcome with guilt about their relationship with God. They suffer from an Atlas complex, thinking the weight of the world is on them. In their minds, it's up to them to remain obedient, faithful, and in good standing with God. If they fail God too much, they may lose their salvation. If they find their moral strength failing them, they fear the consequences could be eternal. So with flexed, tense muscles and sweat on their brow, they live life suspending their salvation on their shoulders.

This new contract is about God's promise to himself.

Every Christian I've met who believes they can lose their salvation has always given a reason that involves *them*. What if *I* commit suicide? What if *I* get a divorce? What if *I* stop believing? What if *I* . . . ? You fill in the blank there, but it's all the same. Every hypothetical scenario puts ourselves at the center of the equation.

But our faithfulness to God is an *old*-covenant problem that is solved by the new. Under the new, God has accomplished the unthinkable: he has taken us out of the equation. Our salvation and our faithfulness are all about him:

> If we are faithless,
>   he will remain faithful,
>   for he cannot disown himself. (2 Tim. 2:13)

Even our spiritual growth is about him:

> He who *began* a good work in you *will carry it on to completion.* (Phil. 1:6)

> The head, from whom the entire body, being supplied and held together by the joints and ligaments, grows *with a growth which is from God.* (Col. 2:19 NASB)

Religion tells us that we're at the heart of the equation. We must "do." And we're never done until we hit heaven and find out if it was enough. In contrast, this new way is all about what Jesus *has done* to provide an unbreakable connection with God and guaranteed growth in him.

God's new way is not about us. It's all about him. And God's new way allows us to embark on the lifelong adventure of knowing Jesus intimately, *without* any religion to kill it.

3

One day as I walked down the hall at the University of Notre Dame, I heard a conversation I'll never forget. Just as I passed by a classroom door, a student asked her professor, "Why was God so different toward people in the Old Testament?"

It was a religion class taught by a priest, and the student was asking a question I was very interested in. So I stopped dead in my tracks to listen.

"God didn't treat people *that* differently in the Old Testament," the priest answered. "The Old Testament and the New Testament are quite similar in how they portray God's interactions with us."

The student seemed puzzled by the answer. But since the professor was a priest, she figured a priest was an expert. I watched her scribble down some notes as the priest moved on to his next point.

Would you agree that God interacts with people similarly in the Old and New Testaments? Sure, God himself hasn't changed. But as we've seen, the contract by which he relates to us is *very* different. A line of some sort has been drawn. To ignore this is to miss the whole point of Jesus bursting on the scene.

Under the old way, God grew angry at Israel for their sins. Under the new way, we are saved from God's anger (Rom. 5:9). Under the old, people were burdened with yearly reminders of their sins. Under the new, God remembers our sins no more (Heb. 8:12). Under the old, the Holy Spirit came upon people temporarily for times of service. Under the new, God's Spirit lives in us forever (Eph. 1:13–14). Under the old, David pleaded with God so that he wouldn't remove his Spirit. Under the new, God has made us one spirit with him (1 Cor. 6:17). And he'll never leave us (Heb. 13:5).

The way we relate to God is *very* different today. There's been a system change that has made the old way obsolete (Heb. 7:12; 8:8–9). It's now been totally set aside, because it was "weak" and "useless" and could never make anyone right with God (Heb. 7:18–19; 8:13; 10:8–10). Consequently, there's only one thing we should be ministering to the church today—the *new* covenant, nothing else:

> He has made us competent as *ministers of a new covenant—not of the letter* but of the Spirit; for the letter kills, but the Spirit gives life. (2 Cor. 3:6)

"Shoplifter! Shoplifter!"

"We've got him on tape! We caught him red-handed!" I said to Aidan's father. But he wasn't impressed. "Why would you do this to Aidan? What kind of friend are you to him?" he asked.

I was stunned. I'd imagined Aidan's father would be proud of us for investigating his son's behavior and collecting the evidence. My friend Tony and I were in junior high, and we were attending a church our parents founded. We saw ourselves as owners, perhaps even young leaders in the church, even at an early age. We were full of pride and religion and had devised a plan to trap one of our own friends in his wrongdoing.

I brought the tape recorder, and Tony asked the questions. If we could just get Aidan to admit to shoplifting, we'd surely be rewarded.

The Sunday school hour ended, and we had fifteen minutes before the service. All of us kids went down to the convenience store to get snacks and drinks. Our hope was that Aidan would once again show off his shoplifting prowess. This time, we were ready to catch him in the act!

Sure enough, Aidan walked away from the store that morning with "free" goodies in his coat pocket. "What do you have there, Aidan?" Tony asked. Meanwhile, I held my arm out in Aidan's direction. (I had something secret of my own tucked away in my coat sleeve—the tape recorder!)

By the time we returned to church, we had the evidence we needed. Aidan admitted not only to shoplifting that morning but also to similar crimes in the past.

"Boy, will Aidan's dad be proud of us for straightening Aidan out!" we thought. But after playing the tape for Aidan's dad and getting his furious response, Tony and

I could only exchange a befuddled look. How could this have gone wrong? Why weren't we the heroes?

Deep down, we knew Aidan's father was right. I mean, what had we really accomplished? Nothing we'd done was in love. And the result was that Aidan wouldn't talk to us for months. We had severed our relationship with him as we sought to "convict" him.

Looking back on the way we treated Aidan reminds me of what happens to people under law. We become cold, hard, and judgmental. And we begin collecting evidence against one another, all the while sinning against the very same law we claim to keep:

> *You who preach against stealing*, do you steal? You who say that people should not commit adultery, do you commit adultery? You who abhor idols, do you rob temples? *You who brag about the law, do you dishonor God by breaking the law?* As it is written: "God's name is blasphemed among the Gentiles because of you." (Rom. 2:21–24)

THE PROBLEM WITH THE OLD

So what *exactly* is the problem with the old way? The law points its holy finger at us and silences every one of us. Through the law, we only become more aware of our sin:

> Now we know that whatever the law says, it says to those who are under the law, *so that every mouth may be silenced* and the whole world held accountable to God. Therefore no one will be declared righteous in his sight by observing the law; rather, *through the law we become conscious of sin*. (Rom. 3:19–20)

The law craftily paints us into a corner, showing us that we're trapped as prisoners of sin (Gal. 3:19–24). After showing us our sin, the law offers us no real solution. The law can't give new birth, new life, or even hope for these in the near future (Gal. 2:16; 3:21).

The law points its holy finger at us and silences every one of us.

Being under law is like being under a curse (Gal. 3:10). The demands of the law aren't difficult; they're impossible! At the same time that the law is screaming, "Thou shalt not sin!" its regulations actually *arouse* more sin within us (Rom. 7:5). So there we are with no hope to meet the standard and things only getting worse by the minute.

Because the law gives sin the opportunity to thrive (Rom. 7:8), it becomes a ministry of condemnation (2 Cor. 3:7). Yes, God brought the law in so that our sins would *increase*, not decrease:

> The Law came in *so that the transgression would increase*; but where sin increased, grace abounded all the more. (Rom 5:20 NASB)

If anyone is looking to the old way of the law for answers, they can expect *more* sinning, not less. Have you ever considered that the religious demands you place on yourself might actually be the *cause* of your sin struggle? It seems the only way we can experience relief while under law is by bending its rules when people aren't looking. But as we'll see next, some end up parading their disobedience right through the center of town!

MENNONITE MOTORBOAT

While living in northern Indiana, we learned a lot about Mennonite culture. In that area, there are three main types of Mennonites. One of the easiest ways to distinguish them is by their modes of transportation. Some refrain from driving cars altogether. Others drive only a black car with no shiny trim. And a third group drives any car they want.

South of town, there was an intersection with churches on three corners. Driving by on Sunday, you got a perfect snapshot of all three Mennonite viewpoints. One parking lot had cars of all colors and types. The second parking lot was filled with very conservative black cars. And the third parking lot was dirt, with a hitching post for horse-drawn buggies. That last group has decided to refrain from most things in the modern world.

One day, while visiting the local Mennonite town, my wife and I witnessed a scene we'll never forget. A horse drawing a carriage was trotting through the middle of downtown . . . towing a bright yellow speedboat!

We laughed and laughed at the hypocrisy of it all. Yes, the Mennonite man was obeying the letter of Mennonite law. But he had found a loophole of sorts that enabled him to enjoy just a bit of weekend "freedom."

Similarly, the old way of religion tells us exactly where the boundaries are. But when its rules become inconvenient for us, we might find ourselves altering them to fit our desired lifestyle. That way we never confront the stringency of law, and we don't suffer under the full power of its condemnation.

Don't want to live under six-hundred-plus laws of the Old Testament? Then maybe settle on Eleven

Commandments—the Big Ten plus a 10 percent tithe. Don't want to be bound by a required 10 percent? Okay, we're down to just the Ten Commandments. Don't feel like refraining from Friday night emails and Saturday yard work on the Sabbath? Okay, now we're down to the Nine Commandments. As we whittle away at the law to get it the way we like it—nice and palatable—we wallow in the confusion of religion. We also confuse those around us as we fail to rest in the beautiful simplicity of God's new way.

> **Picking and choosing is not really the way the law works.**

Picking and choosing is not really the way the law works. It's actually an all-or-nothing proposition:

> All who rely on observing the law are *under a curse*, for it is written: "Cursed is everyone who does not continue to do *everything* written in the Book of the Law." (Gal. 3:10)

> For whoever keeps the whole law and yet stumbles at just *one point* is guilty of breaking *all* of it. (James 2:10)

Even if we keep the whole law and mess up in just one tiny way, we're cursed for it! So this means we either acknowledge our failure, or we paint the illusion that we're on our way to greatness.

The choice is ours.

Once we realize the hopelessness under the old way, we can engage in a border crossing. We can abandon religion and cross over to experience God without religion. And God shares a counterintuitive secret with us: if we jettison the old way of rules, sin actually *loses* its grip on us:

But sin, seizing *the opportunity afforded by the commandment*, produced in me every kind of covetous desire. For
apart from law, sin is dead. (Rom. 7:8)

Commandments give sin an opportunity. But apart from
law, sin is dead. Apparently, being free from the law and
being free from sin's power go hand in hand. They're prac-
tically one and the same.

But how do we cross the border and leave the old way of
the law *entirely* behind? For that, we now go to live footage
in the woods just outside of France.

4

As the carriage comes to a halt, the Austrian ambassador announces they've arrived at the hand-over ceremony. Marie Antoinette exits the carriage with her dog held tightly to her chest and walks toward a well-decorated tent off the wooded path. There she's met by a French countess who tells her it's time to leave behind everything of her former life in Austria. The countess says she'll be delivered to representatives of the French Court, and she is to embrace an entirely new life in France. Marie waves good-bye to the Austrian ambassador and ducks into the tent with the countess.

Once in the tent, the countess takes her dog away, asking an aide to return it to the Austrians. Marie is then stripped down. Her Austrian clothes are replaced with the finest in French fashion. "The bride must not keep anything from her prior court," the countess says.

At that very moment, Marie is engaged to be married to the Dauphin of France, heir to the French throne. Marie is now French royalty, and there's no place for former things in her life. Her upcoming marriage requires her to break free from all things Austria.

And there's no returning.

Like Marie Antoinette, it's through marriage that we make a clean break from the old way of religion. Prior to meeting Jesus, we were told that religion is a good thing and that we should do our best to abide by its rules. But now we've been married to Jesus Christ. Like Marie, we've become royalty (1 Pet. 2:9). This means our former affection for religion has no place in God's kingdom:

> Therefore, my brethren, you also were made to *die to the Law* through the body of Christ, so that you might be *joined to another*, to Him who was raised from the dead, in order that we might bear fruit for God. (Rom. 7:4 NASB)

Imagine if Marie Antoinette had asked the French Court for permission to wear her old Austrian clothes alongside her new French fashions. Imagine if she'd asked to incorporate her Austrian practices alongside the new ways of France. You can bet the French would have frowned on that idea! Well, the apostle Paul did more than frown on the idea of mixing the old with the new. He actually resorted to name-calling. He said, "You foolish Galatians" (Gal. 3:1) to those who tried to mix the old way of the law with their new life in Christ. Does it sound like God is interested in a mix of old and new?

Our marriage to Jesus means we crossed the border from death to life. As with Marie Antoinette, our border crossing requires a clean break from the old way. Our relationship with the law is over:

> *Christ is the end of the law* so that there may be righteousness for everyone who believes. (Rom. 10:4)

TOO SIMPLE?

Some teach that we Christians are free from the *dietary* rules and *sacrifices* of the law, but we still need the Ten Commandments. Now, let me be quick to say that I don't advocate lying, adultery, or murder. Nor do any Christians that I know, for that matter. But the question is, once we Christians have recognized that law can't save us, should the Ten Commandments still be our *guide* for daily living?

The answer, I believe, is no. A Christian should have *no spiritual relationship of any kind* with the Ten Commandments. Why not? First, many of us don't know what we're saying when we think we're living by the Ten Commandments. If we truly were, we'd abide by the Sabbath, refraining from work Friday evening through Saturday. This is remembering the Sabbath day and keeping it holy—one of the Ten Commandments.

Some will say, "Well, we're free from the Sabbath. That's different!" My reply is, "So then it's the *Nine* Commandments that we're under?" I don't see in Scripture where we're told we can dice up God's law into segments—sacrificial, dietary, moral, and Sabbath—in order to get it the way we like it. As we've seen, the law is an

> Our relationship with the law is over.

all-or-nothing proposition (James 2:10). We can't adopt just *some* of it.

The apostle Paul says we're cursed if we don't do *everything* written in the law (Gal. 3:10). This is precisely why God freed us from *all* requirements of the law, not just some. We don't have the right to cherry-pick, selecting the parts that are comfortable for us. Choosing to abide by part of the law, whether it's 1 percent or 99 percent or anywhere in between, is not an option. If we take on the business of law keeping, we're required to keep the *whole* law. And if we adopt the law even as *part* of our belief system, Jesus becomes of "no benefit" to us at all (Gal. 5:2–4 NASB).

THE BIG TEN TOO?

But maybe this "freedom from the law" talk doesn't apply to the Ten Commandments. Maybe this is too radical, an overreaction to legalism. After all, where does it say the Ten Commandments themselves bring condemnation and struggle? I'm glad you asked. There are two passages that are convincing to me. Here's the first:

> Now if *the ministry that brought death*, which was *engraved in letters on stone*, came with glory, so that the Israelites could not look steadily at the face of Moses because of its glory, fading though it was, will not the ministry of the Spirit be even more glorious? If *the ministry that condemns* men is glorious, how much more glorious is the ministry that brings righteousness! For what was glorious *has no glory now* in comparison with the surpassing glory. And if what *was fading away* came

with glory, how much greater is the glory of that which lasts! (2 Cor. 3:7–11)

Paul refers to the law as "the ministry that brought death, which was engraved in letters on stone" (2 Cor. 3:7). That last bit about being engraved in letters on stone was true *only* of the Ten Commandments. The rest of the law was not written on stone—only the Ten.

First, Paul says the Ten Commandments minister death. Second, he says the Ten Commandments condemn. Third, he says the ministry of the Ten Commandments only had a fading glory. This passage is fairly convincing that we Christians shouldn't look to the Ten Commandments as our source or guide. There's a new ministry of the Spirit today, which has a greater glory!

But it's not just that the Ten Commandments point out sins we *already* struggle with. When we place ourselves under the Big Ten, our flesh bolts into action. And the result? We end up setting world records for sin. In Romans 7, Paul reveals that the law gave sin an opportunity to be *aroused* (not stifled!) within him:

> For while we were in the flesh, *the sinful passions, which were aroused by the Law*, were at work in the members of our body to bear fruit for death. . . . But sin, taking *opportunity through the commandment*, produced in me coveting of every kind; for apart from the Law sin is dead. (Rom. 7:5, 8 NASB)

What kind of sin did Paul struggle with under law? The sin of coveting. So *which commandment* was bringing Paul to his knees? "Thou shall not covet"—one of the Ten. So even the Ten Commandments stir up "coveting of every kind" (Rom. 7:8 NASB). Do we expect a different result than the apostle Paul got as we use the Ten Commandments as a source for godly living?

Paul concludes that "apart from the Law sin is dead" (Rom. 7:8 NASB). In this context, he means that apart from the Ten Commandments (specifically "Thou shall not covet"), sin is dead. So if we Christians hope for victory over sin, we shouldn't have *any* relationship with the law, not even the Big Ten. If we hang on to the law as our guide, we can expect sin, guilt, and a whole lot of confusion.

> If we hang on to the law as our guide, we can expect sin, guilt, and a whole lot of confusion.

The law is ineffective to save us. It's ineffective to grow us. It's just plain ineffective for believers (Heb. 7:18). We have no practical, everyday use for it as a guide in our Christian lives.

For us, it's now obsolete (Heb. 8:13).

Good for Nothing?

But isn't the law still good for something? After all, in Matthew 5, Jesus said he did *not* come to abolish the law:

> Do not think that I have come to abolish the Law or the Prophets; I have not come to abolish them but to fulfill them. I tell you the truth, *until heaven and earth disappear*, not the smallest letter, not the least stroke of a pen, will by any means disappear from the Law *until everything is accomplished*. (Matt. 5:17–18)

Last time I checked, heaven and earth were still here. So the law is still around too—it's *not* abolished. But if the law doesn't help us Christians live upright lives, then what use is it?

Of course the law is still useful today. The law has a specific purpose on this side of the cross. But apparently we're not the first to misunderstand that purpose:

> They want to be teachers of the law, but they do not know what they are talking about or what they so confidently affirm. We know that the law is good if one uses it *properly*. We also know that law is made *not for the righteous* but for lawbreakers and rebels, the ungodly and sinful, the unholy and irreligious; for those who kill their fathers or mothers, for murderers. (1 Tim. 1:7–9)

Here, Paul tells the young pastor Timothy that he should beware of those that misapply the law to Christians ("the righteous"). So if the law isn't for believers, there's only one other group it *can* be for:

> *Before this faith came*, we were held prisoners by the law, locked up until faith should be revealed. So *the law was put in charge to lead us to Christ* that we might be justified by faith. Now that faith has come, we are no longer under the supervision of the law. (Gal. 3:23–25)

The law tutors us as *unbelievers*, showing us our sin. But once we come to faith in Jesus, we no longer have use for the law. Christians are not under the law and not to be supervised by the law after salvation (Gal. 3:25; 5:18; Rom. 6:14).

The Ten Commandments and other moral laws, even as understood intuitively by our consciences, are essential to nonbelievers. These standards point out how every one of us is born with an addiction to sin: "The requirements of the law are written on their hearts, their *consciences* also bearing witness, and their thoughts now accusing, now even defending them" (Rom. 2:15). The law accuses us, and we attempt to defend ourselves. We live the best we can. But once we admit our guilt and cross over into new life in Jesus, our relationship with the law is over. We enter into that new contract with God. We're ready for the new way of the Spirit.

The law tutors us as *unbelievers,* showing us our sin.

MAKING IT PERSONAL

Does a clean break from law religion sound too simplistic? Well, I hope it sounds simplistic, because it *should* be simple. Jesus said we should approach the kingdom of God like little children (Mark 10:15). And Paul was afraid the early church would stray from the simplicity of the new way and make things complicated (2 Cor. 11:3).

For us, it's a simple choice. It's six-hundred-plus Jewish commands and regulations, or it's total freedom to "serve in the new way of the Spirit, and not in the old way of the written code" (Rom. 7:6). But there's no room for selecting from the law and imposing a few things here and there. That makes no sense at all!

In personalizing this message of "God without religion," here are some truths we need to come to grips with:

- I'm dead to the law (Rom. 7:4; Gal. 2:19).
- I'm not under the law (Rom. 6:14).

- I'm free from the law (Rom. 6:7).
- I'm not supervised by the law (Gal. 3:25).
- I don't serve in the old way of the law (Rom. 7:6).
- I can live in the newness and freedom of the Spirit (Rom. 7:6; Gal. 5:13).

These truths shout a black-and-white reality. Yes, the law, including the Ten Commandments, is "holy, righteous and good" (Rom. 7:12). The law is so perfect that nobody can live up to it. Because of its perfection, it's designed to make sin thrive. That's how it points us to Jesus for salvation. But once we come to Jesus, we need to go ahead and make it personal.

"Christ is the end of the law" *for me* (Rom. 10:4).

5

Recently the United States completed a lengthy presidential election campaign. Over the course of the year-long campaign, I heard dozens of hours of persuasive rhetoric. Yet not once did any of the candidates address the most important issue to me personally—freedom from the British.

I kept waiting for some candidate to utter the words I longed to hear: "The oppression that we presently endure can no longer be tolerated. We must seek independence. We must obtain the freedom we so desperately sought upon our landing on these foreign, now familiar shores!"

Of course, I'm kidding. We're all aware of where we stand with England. Our struggle with them is ancient history. But I could definitely see a speech like this being given in the mid-1700s. It's a perfect fit for that time and audience.

History matters. Audience is important. And context is key. But often we'll read the Bible, a collection of ancient documents, without considering history, audience, and context. That's dangerous, since we can end up applying things wrongly. Even worse, we might miss the whole point. History, audience, and context are everything as we look back on the Old Testament law.

STOPPING HITCHCOCK

Imagine reading a Stephen King novel but putting it down thirty pages shy of the end and walking away. Imagine watching an Alfred Hitchcock film and turning it off with just a few minutes to go. In both cases, it's possible that you'll miss out on the most important revelation in the whole story! And the surprise ending might mean you need to go back and reinterpret all previous events in light of what you now know.

This is certainly the case with the Bible too. We shouldn't read the Old Testament without placing it in the context of the "surprise ending" of the New. Otherwise, it's very much like laying that novel down thirty pages shy of the end or turning that movie off with just a few minutes to go.

We see the Old in light of the New.

We need to read and study the Old Testament in light of the fact that Jesus came on the scene and fulfilled the law. We see the Old in light of the New. Only then are we teaching the Old in the way God intends—as a covenant that is now "obsolete" (Heb. 8:13) in light of the surpassing glory of the New: "For what was glorious *has no glory now in comparison* with the surpassing glory" (2 Cor. 3:10).

GENTILE ROLL CALL

Are you Jewish by blood? Is your family of Jewish blood-line? If not, you're what the Bible calls a Gentile. For thousands of years, God divided humanity into two main categories—Jew and Gentile.

Why is this important? Because the law was never given to the Gentile. It was never our privilege. No, the law was what distinguished Israel from the rest of the planet. Everyone else was "*excluded* from citizenship in Israel and *foreigners to the covenants of the promise*, without hope and *without God* in the world" (Eph. 2:12).

For a Jewish person to abandon the old way of the law and adopt God's new way was a challenge. We see evidence of that struggle in Hebrews, for example. Hebrews contains thousands of words urging the Jews to jettison the old and hang on tightly to the new. But for most of us, that's not our situation. We're Gentiles. We were never offered the law. Today, we Gentiles are offered one covenant—the new. Breaking free from the old shouldn't really be necessary, *since the old was never really ours to begin with*!

Have you ever thought about that? You, your heritage, your family line—none of it had anything to do with the law if you're a Gentile. And it was the same for the Greeks back then. They had no relationship with the Jewish law. So did Paul march into Galatia or Corinth with the law of Moses under his arm to fix them up? Of course not! If he had, many would have reacted with "Moses who?"

Bringing the law into the picture was the very thing that made Paul angry. Judaizers were following on Paul's heels with a message of "Jesus plus the law." That's exactly what we still hear today: Jesus for salvation and the law for daily living. But the truth is that Gentiles (that's most of us!) were never even offered the law. For us, it's the new covenant or nothing at all.

MULTIPLE CHOICE

Saying that rules, the law, and especially the Ten Commandments have nothing to do with the Christian life appears to be a radical statement these days. Make no mistake—I'm very aware of that. Of all the messages I deliver, this is the one that raises the most eyebrows.

For us, it's the new covenant or nothing at all.

Many of us are still undecided regarding the role of the law in our lives. Before we continue, maybe you should consider where you currently fall in your beliefs about Christians and the law. Consider this statement and check all that apply.

Christians should look to the law . . .

☐ for salvation
☐ as a moral compass
☐ to define sin
☐ for growth in Christ
☐ for none of the above

Now that you've considered the possibilities, let's examine each one. The first one—that we're saved by law—is easy to dismiss. Many passages tell us that no one will be made right with God through the law (Acts 13:39; Rom. 3:28; Gal. 2:16; 3:11). Our initial step into Christ Jesus is unrelated to the law. We're saved by faith, not by observing the law (Gal. 3:24). But the other statements aren't as easy to address. Shouldn't the law be our moral compass that helps us define sin or grow in Christ?

REWRITING SCRIPTURE

Some say Christians should have no relationship with the law for salvation, but we should look to the law as a compass to define sin and keep us on track. Is this right? Let's begin with what we've already seen:

- We're dead to the law (Gal. 2:19; Rom. 7:4).
- We're not under the law (Rom. 6:14).
- We're free from the law (Rom. 6:7).
- We're not supervised by the law (Gal. 3:25).
- We don't serve in the old way of the law (Rom. 7:6).
- We can live in the newness and freedom of the Spirit (Rom. 7:6; Gal. 5:13).

Apparently we don't need the law for dealing with sin or for living uprightly. If we Christians think we need the law to define sin, we forget that *the law defines sin in more than six hundred ways*. Eating pork is sin. Eating shellfish is sin. Saturday mowing is sin—and that's one of the Big Ten. Should we just pick a few that we prefer as our moral guide? There again, we're dicing up

God's law to get it the way we like it. We're deciding that an arbitrarily selected portion of the Mosaic law should be our *source* for defining sin and guiding us toward godliness.

So one popular view is that the law, or a select part of it, is needed as a moral guide for the Christian's daily life. The other view is that the Christian should have no relationship with the law after salvation. *Only one of these two views can possibly be scriptural.* The other view shouldn't find support and should require a virtual rewriting of Scripture.

As I see it, to claim the law guides a Christian's daily life requires a rewriting of Scripture. It means taking the passages we just reviewed and adding the phrase "for salvation" to each. Examples of this rewriting of Scripture would be: "we're dead to the law *for salvation*" or "we're free from the law *for salvation*." By tacking on this phrase, we argue that Christians still need the law as a guide after salvation. Essentially, these theological gymnastics display our lack of confidence in the indwelling Christ to counsel us toward upright living.

The phrase "for salvation" isn't there. No, the Bible plainly says we're dead to the law; we're not under the law; we're free from the law; we're not supervised by the law; and Christ is the end of the law. This is the most straightforward takeaway from these passages. There's no sign of the apostle Paul watering down this radical message. Plain and simple, the law is *not* a compass, a guide, or help toward spiritual growth for the Christian—"if you are *led by* the Spirit, you are not under law" (Gal. 5:18).

SUCKERS FOR RELIGION

According to research conducted by the Barna Group, most Christians equate spiritual maturity with following the rules. About 81 percent of self-identified Christians think that spiritual health is "trying hard to follow the rules described in the Bible." *Even among Christians who realize that salvation isn't earned through good works*, four out of five think that spiritual maturity is "trying hard to follow the rules." Is this what spiritual health and maturity are about?

Is this what spiritual health and maturity are about?

Paul called the Galatians "foolish" for using the law for daily living after salvation (Gal. 3:1). He thought having a relationship with the law after salvation was like spiritual adultery after being married to Jesus (Rom. 7:4; Gal. 5:4). He even confronted the Colossians about their reliance on "Do not" rules instead of depending on Jesus alone for daily living:

> "Do not handle! Do not taste! Do not touch!" . . . Such regulations indeed have *an appearance of wisdom*, with their self-imposed worship, their false humility and their harsh treatment of the body, but *they lack any value* in restraining sensual indulgence. (Col. 2:21, 23)

Paul warned them about the futility of trying to improve themselves by rules. But remember that these were *Gentiles*, just like most of us today. The idea that Christians, especially Gentiles, would return to any portion of the law as our guide for daily living is nothing short of absurd. Why did Paul even have to warn them of the dangers of returning to law? Because addiction to law-based religion isn't just a Jewish problem. It's up close and personal.

We humans are suckers for religion.

6

During my teenage years, I struggled with following the speed limit. Between the ages of sixteen and eighteen, I received a number of traffic tickets for excessive speed. My parents would take away my driving privileges for a month here or there. They'd warn me of the dangers of driving fast. They'd remind me that I could lose my license. Still, I didn't listen and continued to get speeding ticket after speeding ticket. I wasted lots of money and put myself and others in danger.

Many years later, my father and I participated in the Richard Petty Driving Experience at Indianapolis Motor Speedway. First we went through a stock car training class. Then they turned us loose on the Indy 500 track. The drivers who were in line in front of me were turning in speeds of more than 160 miles per hour.

Wow! I thought. *This is what I've always wanted! No tickets, no limits. I can drive as fast as I want!*

Interestingly, though, as I got out onto the track and put the pedal to the metal, I started thinking some surprising thoughts: *I should be careful. The wall is only a few feet away. I don't want to do something stupid and hurt myself or this car. I'll play it safe and just have a good time out here.*

After several laps, my fastest speed was 132 miles per hour. That was slower than a lot of the other drivers. And, ironically, it was slower than some speeds I'd reached as a teenager out on America's highways! Why so conservative on the Indy 500 track? I'm not exactly sure, but I think the fact that it wasn't illegal to go fast made it less appealing. Once the sky was the limit, I could truly decide for myself.

Laws and rules actually cause sin to increase, not decrease. Laws *arouse* sinful passions (Rom. 5:20; 7:5). As we saw, even rules, although they have the appearance of curbing sin, don't really restrain us (Col. 2:20–23). In fact, God tells us, "For sin shall not be your master, *because you are not under law*, but under grace" (Rom. 6:14).

God wasn't acting blindly when he liberated us from the law. He did it for a reason: so that, by the Spirit of his Son in us, we might live a life the law could never give. He invites us to a life freely chosen, not one of duty or obligation. Just as I chose freely out there on the Indy 500 track, we are intended to live out the idea that "everything is permissible, but not everything is beneficial" (1 Cor. 6:12; 10:23). When the sky's the limit, we discover what we *really* want.

"A New Command I Give You"

Maybe the Ten Commandments and the rest of the law have no bearing on the lives of Christians today. Still, it's clear from Scripture that *some kind* of laws are written in Christians' hearts, right?

Yes, there are laws written in our hearts. But here's the fundamental question: What exactly *are* those laws?

First, remember that Jesus tells us that the two greatest commandments *in the law* are to love God and to love others. In these two, Jesus says, all the law and all the prophets are fulfilled (Matt. 22:37–40). From this, we know that *love has historically been what's most important in God's eyes.*

When the sky's the limit, we discover what we *really* want.

In the Epistles, James tells us that the "royal law" is loving others (James 2:8). Similarly, Paul tells us that *all* of the moral concerns in the Ten Commandments are summed up in the idea of loving others (Rom. 13:8–10). And the apostle Peter wrote, "Above all, love each other deeply, because *love covers over a multitude of sins*" (1 Peter 4:8).

So love is key. But is it the *Mosaic* laws of "love the LORD your God with all your heart and with all your soul and with all your strength" (Deut. 6:5) and "love your neighbor as yourself" (Lev. 19:18) that are in our hearts?

Actually, no.

We just saw that these two are the greatest commandments *in the law*. But if these laws were written in our hearts today, God would be sending us a mixed message about the law. He'd be saying that *part* of the Mosaic law is still for us today. Yes, it's true that love is key. And yes, it's true that love is written in our hearts. But notice *exactly* how Jesus puts it:

> A *new command* I give you: Love one another. *As I have loved you*, so you must love one another. (John 13:34)

Jesus was talking to a Jewish audience. They were well aware of the commands in the law about loving God and loving others. But they were used to hearing they should love others *as they love themselves*. Here, Jesus announces that he's introducing them to a new command, one they've never heard before!

This new command involves *grasping how much God loves us* and *transmitting that same love* to others. Jesus's command is greater than any love command his audience encountered in the writings of Moses. It's one thing to love others the way that you love yourself. It's a wholly different thing to love others with the very same love with which God loves you!

It's all about believing in Jesus and transmitting *his* love to others.

The apostle John confirms what Jesus's commands are today:

> And this is his command: *to believe* in the name of his Son, Jesus Christ, and *to love* one another *as he commanded us*. (1 John 3:23)

John says to love one another as Jesus commanded us. How did Jesus command us to love? While the law said "love your neighbor as yourself" (Lev. 19:18), Jesus said to love others "as I have loved you" (John 13:34).

The bottom line is this: today, it's all about believing in Jesus and transmitting *his* love to others. That's what's written in our hearts, *not* the law of Moses.

BEHAVIOR VERSES

But what's the difference between all those New Testament behavior verses and the old way of rules and regulations? The difference, I believe, can be summed up in one simple question: "What if I don't comply?"

Under the law, disobedience brought severe consequences. On an individual level, for example, sexual sins and idolatry were punishable by death. Other punishments involved banishment, removal of limbs, and other severe penalties. Because of their sins, Israel severed their connection with God again and again. God punished them with war, exile, and even death. In contrast, we Christians have been told that all things are permissible. All things? Yes, but not all things are beneficial. Paul actually writes this *twice* in the same letter (1 Cor. 6:12; 10:23).

Our motivation for making good choices should not be fear of punishment. There are indeed consequences, certainly. If we lie, we'll spend our lives looking over our shoulder. When we do hurtful things to each other, we damage relationships. When we make poor choices, we live with the results. When we break the laws of the land, we suffer legal consequences.

But God will not punish Christians. All the punishment God had for us in response to our sins was laid on Jesus (1 Pet. 2:24). There is none left (Rom. 8:1; Heb. 9:28). So

New Testament behavior verses aren't laws that must be kept for fear of punishment. They are advice given by a loving Father regarding what is constructive and beneficial.

At first glance, sin may appear to offer us a Fourth of July experience, fireworks and all. But the next day, there we are out in the field picking up all the trash we left behind. This is precisely why Paul asks us this question:

> Therefore *what benefit* were you then deriving from the things of which you are now ashamed? For *the outcome* of those things is death. (Rom. 6:21 NASB)

Paul's focus is on the absence of any real *benefit* from sin. He notes the *outcome* of foolish choices. Who wants to waste time sinning and fighting the shame when we have the privilege of participating in God's divine nature (2 Pet. 1:4) and expressing Christ himself?

WHAT NOT TO WEAR

One popular television program of recent years is *What Not to Wear*. Based in New York City, this program features Stacy and Clinton, the two cohosts who enter people's homes, raid their closets, and tell them what "works" and what doesn't. In particular, they're skilled at showing people the fashions that look good on them based on their body type.

Men and women all over the USA are on the waiting list to get advice from Stacy and Clinton—advice they feel will make them better looking and more appealing to others. As a result, they'll feel better about themselves.

Behavior verses in the New Testament aren't m̶
ferent from the advice that Stacy and Clinton give. We ι̶
told to "put on love" and "put on Christ" and "put on
compassion" much like the guests on the TV show are
told what to wear. In addition, we're told to toss away attitudes and behaviors that aren't profitable, just as Stacy
and Clinton hold up certain outfits to the mirror and then
toss them aside, saying, "That looks awful!"

Some clothes simply don't fit, while others fit just right
and look great. In the same way, some attitudes and behaviors are not "fitting for saints" (Eph. 5:3 NKJV), while
others are the perfect fit for God's children.

Does this sound like religion to you? It's **Who doesn't
want to travel in
heavenly style?** not in the least! Throughout the Epistles,
we're just discovering the most fashionable
way for saints to dress. And, hey, who doesn't
want to travel in heavenly style?

So next time you come across that passage in Ephesians
or Romans or wherever about "what to do," remember your
identity as a child of God. With that in mind, know that
God is simply pointing out the clothes that fit you well:

> Therefore, as God's chosen people, holy and dearly loved,
> *clothe yourselves* with compassion, kindness, humility,
> gentleness and patience. (Col. 3:12)

PART 2

DIVINE SLOT MACHINE?

Tithing changes our giving from the realm of voluntary worship to that of slavish obedience to law.
John Harvey Grime (1851–1941)

7

We'd been attending a church for about a year when an outside consultant was called in to lead fundraising for a building project. We were introduced to the consultant during a Sunday morning service. He took about twenty minutes to distribute a survey asking us what we give, who we give to, and why we give to them. After the surveys were collected, the consultant began visiting the adult education classes and home groups.

When he reached our group, it was obvious that he was comfortable with his material and smooth in his delivery. He began by telling us about our church's building project and the fundraising campaign. Then he transitioned into a story.

"I knew a man in a church with a fundraising campaign much like this one. This man found himself hesitant to give to his church, because his daughter was ill. He was overwhelmed with her medical bills. Month after month, he watched as his daughter's health declined and the bills mounted. Meanwhile, the church struggled in raising funds.

"Finally, the man was convicted and decided to step out in faith by tithing 10 percent to his church. Despite his growing debt, he pledged to support his church no matter what. Once he began tithing, his daughter's health began to improve. And eventually she completely recovered!

"God is indeed faithful when we are faithful to him. We need to get out of our comfort zones and give, even when it hurts."

Then the consultant invited us to make a "pledge" for our church. He assured us that God would bless us in return.

The message was that we could *buy* God's blessings in our lives.

As you read the story about the father and his sick daughter, you may have picked up on the subtle (or not so subtle) underlying message. The daughter's health only improved *after* her father began tithing. The implication was that we too could experience freedom from difficult circumstances in our lives if we pledged 10 percent. In short, the message was that we could *buy* God's blessings in our lives. Also, reading between the lines, God might withhold his blessing (of healing a loved one, in this case) if we withhold our money from him.

This was a solid church, so we hung tight. We were confident in the discernment of our church leadership. Sure enough, it was only a matter of weeks before cries of "Pressure! Manipulation! Prosperity gospel!" arose in the congregation. Church leadership agreed, and that was the last we saw of the consultant and the fundraising campaign.

MONEY-BACK GUARANTEE

What we experienced during that fundraising campaign was the "light" version of tithing guilt. Some television ministries go a lot further than that. They say, "Anything you give will be returned threefold!" (I've noticed that when they get really desperate, you'll start hearing *seven*fold!) I've often wondered why those ministries don't just give to God's work elsewhere. By the same logic, their television ministries would then receive sevenfold back!

Other churches have offered a money-back guarantee on your tithe. And they even put a time limit on God's payback, saying, "If God doesn't bless you within three months of giving your tithe, we'll refund it!" Now, who's willing to be the guy who approaches them three months later saying, "Our family gave $900 in June, and it's been three months. We haven't been blessed yet"? At that point, you can guess what's coming: "Well, brother, your problem is not what you gave. It's your lack of faith! You need to trust God to bless you, and then he will. He blessed all of *us* after we gave. He'll return a blessing to you as well." Someone else adds, "Think about all the good things that have happened in your life over the last three months. Those *are* God's blessings. You just need to open your eyes to them—they're all around you!"

No one wants to be the guy who "lacked faith." No one wants to appear spiritually blind to God's blessings in their life. So the money-back guarantee on tithing can end up being a real winner for churches.

But where do we get the idea that we can give in full expectation that God's going to pay us back and then some?

And doesn't that take some of the joy out of giving? Paul described those who think along those lines as "men of *corrupt mind*, who have been robbed of the truth and *who think that godliness is a means to financial gain*" (1 Tim. 6:5). Oh, and those money-back guarantee offers are usually accompanied by an Old Testament quote from Malachi:

> "Bring the whole tithe into the storehouse, that there may be food in my house. Test me in this," says the LORD Almighty, "and see if I will not throw open the floodgates of heaven and *pour out so much blessing* that you will not have enough room for it." (Mal. 3:10)

But for very good reason, surrounding verses in Malachi are seldom included in these tithing challenges. Malachi 3:8 says, "You rob me," and verse 9 says, "You are under a curse." Why are these parts left out of the appeal? Because old covenant statements involving curses aren't very marketable these days. It's not exactly "ecclesiastically correct" to go around telling people they're under a curse until they fork over 10 percent of their income. So the sales pitch ends up being only *half* of the Malachi message—the blessing part.

Is this how God operates, with no more discernment than a mindless machine?

The bottom line is that any message that communicates that we pay God money and in return he blesses us financially is flawed (1 Tim. 6:5). Make no bones about it—under this theology, God becomes the Divine Slot Machine. We put our quarters in and pull the faith lever down. If we put enough quarters in and believe hard enough, we'll hit the jackpot.

Is this how God operates, with no more discernment than a mindless machine?

A Carryover?

"I know, we're free from the law. But . . . we should still give 10 percent, since that's carried over from the Old Testament, isn't it?"

I hear questions like this a lot. It's natural to wonder how a pure grace message fits with giving to support the local church. Do we tithe a specific amount? Do we just give whatever we want (or don't want) to give? And how will anybody be motivated to give if it's just a "free-for-all" message of grace?

In response to my first book, *The Naked Gospel*, I received an email warning me in the strongest possible terms that the message of freewill giving under grace would damage America's churches. The message went on to say that my view was "deeply disappointing to those of us studied enough to have figured out the simple truth about giving *10 percent* to God."

I'm no stranger to comments like these. I get them all the time. And since I serve as a pastor at Ecclesia, other pastors wonder how I could take such a position on grace giving and still make it. "How does your church even survive with you teaching this?" they ask.

Finances are one of the most difficult areas for us leaders to deal with today. I have yet to visit a church that has no need for financial support from its congregation. I'm not sure God even wants us to have a church like that. Paul talked frequently about how the churches he visited sup- ported him financially and gave to fellow believers in need. New covenant, grace-based giving is presented as a gift to the giver, not just the receiver. It's healthy and good for us to support our church financially and *other ways* as well:

> We have different gifts, according to the grace given us. If a man's gift is prophesying, let him use it in proportion to his faith. If it is serving, let him serve; if it is teaching, let him teach; if it is encouraging, let him encourage; *if it is contributing to the needs of others, let him give generously*; if it is leadership, let him govern diligently; if it is showing mercy, let him do it cheerfully. (Rom. 12:6–8)

All the same, many pastors and church leaders can fall into the trap of mandating a certain percentage of money from their congregation. Maybe it's not out of any nega- tive motivation. Some are sincerely convinced that this percentage is God-ordained. In the Old Testament, Israel was clearly instructed to give a tenth of everything they had to support the priests. Why would it be any different today? To answer this question, let's take a look at the history of tithing and compare it with what we find about giving under God's new way.

8

In the Old Testament, God divided Israel into twelve tribes. Each tribe received their share of the Promised Land. Well, each tribe except one. One tribe, called the Levites after Joseph's brother Levi, didn't receive any property. In fact, they were instructed to remain free of personal belongings. Why? Because they served a unique purpose as mediators between God and the people. This was a full-time responsibility, so the other tribes were required to support them.

Each tribe gave a tenth to the Levites. This enabled them to serve God in full-time ministry without being concerned about money. But tithing under the law involved *more than just 10 percent* of your income. It also meant contributing grain and other offerings that added up to much more.

So here's a question: If we were supposed to be tithing a mandatory 10 percent today, to whom would it go? The priestly tribe of Levi is gone. Their function as mediators between God and humans is over. And the Bible tells us that our high priest is not our pastor, our minister, a Christian leader, or our church. We have one High Priest, Jesus (Heb. 7:26–28). In addition, *every* member of the body of Christ is a priest (1 Pet. 2:9; Heb. 13:10).

To whom would the tithe go?

So to whom would the tithe go?

We Christians are free from the law. Consequently, we're free from a mandatory 10 percent standard for giving. Tithing is not a system that is in place for us today. *There is not one single instance of instruction in any New Testament epistle for Christians to give a 10 percent tithe.*

"But what does Jesus say about tithing?" you might ask.

In the Gospels, Jesus refers to tithing only three times. Each time, Jesus criticizes the Pharisees because they were beating their chests in pride about their tithing. They thought they were doing well in giving the right amount of money. But Jesus says they were not doing right as they ignored the spirit of the law: justice, mercy, and faithfulness (Luke 11:42; 18:11–14; Matt. 23:23).

MEL'S PLACE

The book of Hebrews *does* mention the term "tithe" (a tenth). It's found in a history lesson about Abraham and his gift to a foreign priest, Melchizedek. Some argue that because Abraham paid a tenth to Melchizedek before the law, the concept of tithing *precedes* the law. Then they suggest that giving 10 percent is a God-given requirement.

They say it's still in effect for today's churches, despite our freedom from the law.

This argument doesn't hold up for three reasons. First, Abraham's gift to Melchizedek was entirely voluntary, not a required command from God. In fact, it was a common practice in the Middle East after winning a battle to give a tenth of your stolen goods to a royal figure out of respect for their position. Second, Abraham gave this tenth only *one time* in his entire life. It was not a regular or habitual giving to Melchizedek. If we Christians were to follow Abraham's act as a model for our giving, it would only be fitting for us to give *once* in our lifetime. Lastly, note that Abraham offered a tenth of his *spoils of war*. In following Abraham's model for giving, it would then be justifiable for Christians to engage in war with other people groups, take their belongings, and then put 10 percent of the loot on the church lawn.

The truth is that Abraham offered a gift to Melchizedek purely *out of respect for his priesthood*. It was a picture of Christ's priesthood to come. This was not a required gift, nor is it an example that we must follow. Instead, Hebrews simply retells this event to show that "the lesser person is blessed by the greater" (Heb. 7:7). This means that Abraham (and Levi, who would descend from him) was lesser than Melchizedek. Therefore, Levi and Old Testament priests are *lesser than Christ*.

This is the logic behind recounting the event. There are no life application verses in this Hebrews passage, meaning there is *no instruction of any kind* for New Testament Christians to give a required tenth. If God had wanted New Testament believers to give exactly a tenth, wouldn't he have put that instruction in at least one epistle?

FREEDOM IN GIVING

From Romans to Revelation, there is no passage that instructs Christians to give a required 10 percent. In fact, we find the opposite—under God's new way, there's no minimum and no maximum. It's entirely up to us:

> Each man should give what he has *decided in his heart* to give, *not reluctantly or under compulsion,* for God loves a *cheerful* giver. (2 Cor. 9:7)

Paul dismisses the idea of pressure ("compulsion") as a reason to give. Rather than embracing the obligation that goes with a tithe ("Give what is right, not what is left," as the church sign says), the church should be the *last* place that puts pressure on people to give.

It's exciting to participate alongside the God of the universe.

So why give? Three good reasons for giving are discussed in the New Testament. First, we're told to give when there's a *need* (2 Cor. 8:12). Next, we're told to share with others when we have *abundance* (2 Cor. 8:13–15). And finally, we see the early church giving because they were *excited* about the message and wanted to see a *spiritual* "harvest" from their giving (2 Cor. 9:7–10). You've got to admit that it's exciting to participate alongside the God of the universe, collaborating in the work that *he* is doing. Now there's a reason to give!

Does It Really "Work"?

As a pastor, I know firsthand how tempting it is to just scoot this whole "freedom from tithing" thing under the rug. Any church leadership would be overjoyed to know they have a guaranteed 10 percent of the church members' income to budget every year. It's all too easy to panic over the perennially short church budget and succumb to some pressure tactics to meet that bottom line.

But how well do those tactics work anyway? A recent survey of churches across America revealed that the average churchgoer gives under 3 percent to their church. And more than half of churchgoers give nothing at all. Despite our leaders' best attempts to motivate, giving is still pretty dismal.

The question we should be asking is *not* "Does freedom in giving really work?" but instead "What does the new covenant teach us about giving?" Then, if what we teach is truth, the result is up to God and *his* church.

But this whole "grace giving" thing can be scary. I'm not going to dodge this issue: you may decide to take this approach with your church or ministry, and it may fail. Your budget could take a nosedive. You may even have to shut the doors. There is no guaranteed success in this approach—in a financial sense, that is.

But we leaders need to ask ourselves a few questions. First, do we believe our all-powerful God is able to secure financial support for something *he* wants to move forward? I think most of us would agree the answer to this one is yes. Now, here's a harder question: If the funds are not coming in, is God really at work there? In some cases, the answer might be yes. But maybe we're just not making the need known or sharing our excitement enough with others. Sadly, though, in some cases the answer to that question might actually be no—even for a ministry dear to our hearts that seems to be meeting a need. So if that's the case, then the last question to ask is this: Do we really want to be pushing a ministry that God does not appear to be motivating people to support?

So to leaders, I'd say this: If we don't have much to lose—a majority aren't giving 10 percent anyway!—why not give new covenant giving a try? We church leaders should be honest about our needs. But we also need to be honest about Christian freedom in giving. If we allow people to think for themselves and give 1 percent, 8 percent, 12 percent, or whatever they truly want, then what might happen?

Why not give new covenant giving a try?

Interestingly, I've found that many people haven't given anything in the past because they felt that if it wasn't 10 percent, then it wouldn't "count." This is the conclusion they arrived at after hearing the required 10 percent tithe message, so they just gave up on the idea of giving. How does the idea of "grace giving" esteem *any* gift and change all that? I guess we leaders will never know until we try.

At our church, I would rather close the doors than encourage "religious" tithing. New Testament giving is to be done from the heart, not under compulsion. We can give based on what we have and based upon the need of the moment. But we shouldn't be reluctant either, just sitting on our wallets. Under grace, we're free to excel in the privilege of giving, no matter what percentage of our income it turns out to be.

That's new covenant freedom in action!

PART **3**

THE TWO MINISTRIES
OF CHRIST

**Self-improvement is both a sin
and an impossibility.**
Norman Grubb (1895–1993)

9

A few years ago I was speaking at a men's retreat in the mountains of West Virginia. The first thing I presented was the importance of the dividing line of the cross—the event that ushered in God's new way. The concept is simple: it's the death of Christ and *not his birth* that initiated the New Testament era (Heb. 9:16–18). Therefore, Jesus was born under the law. And he ministered to an audience *still* under the law (Gal. 4:4–5). This means the New Testament (or new covenant) era didn't begin with "baby Jesus."

"Everyone please turn to Matthew chapter 1," I said.

After they had reached the chapter, I said, "Now flip back just one page and tell me what you see."

"The New Testament," everyone shouted.

"That's right. In most Bibles, there's a divider page that says 'The New Testament' in big block letters. So is that correct? Does the New Testament really begin in Matthew 1? Does the New Testament era start with Jesus as a baby in the manger?"

"No, I guess not," one guy muttered.

I waited a few seconds to let the concept really sink in. Suddenly, I heard a loud ripping noise at the back of the room. The senior pastor of the Baptist church hosting the retreat was holding up a page he'd torn from his Bible. It was the New Testament divider page.

"Guess I won't be needing this anymore!" he announced. Couldn't have said it better myself.

THE GREAT DIVIDE

Baby Jesus, lying in the manger in Bethlehem, was born under law. And all those around him were still under law:

> But when the fullness of the time came, God sent forth His Son, born of a woman, *born under the Law*, so that He might redeem *those who were under the Law*, that we might receive the adoption as sons. (Gal. 4:4–5 NASB)

There it is in black and white—a neglected truth. Yes, we are quite familiar with the idea that Jesus was "born of a woman." But many of us may have lost sight of the fact that Jesus was "born under the Law." This means that in Matthew 1 and throughout the four Gospels, *God's new way had not come on the scene yet*. It was thirty-three years later, at Jesus's *death*, that the new covenant went into effect:

> For where a covenant is, there must of necessity be the death of the one who made it. For *a covenant is valid only when men are dead*, for it is never in force while the one who made it lives. (Heb. 9:16–17 NASB)

Although the divider page in our Bibles tells us that Matthew 1 introduces the New Testament, it's nothing more than a literary convention. It doesn't communicate the truth of the cross as the great divide. Jesus's *death*, not his birth, is what really initiated the New Testament era.

THE FIRST MINISTRY OF CHRIST

The truth concerning this great divide of the cross carries some sweeping implications for how we understand the Bible—the teachings of Jesus in particular—and how we relate to God and live life. So in light of the great divide of the cross, how do we understand the teachings of Jesus?

Throughout his ministry, Jesus focused on two very specific things. His *second* ministry involved prophecy about a new way to come—a way free of rules, regulations, and religion. He spoke of a grace-based system in which we could call God "Daddy." That's usually what comes to our minds when we first think about Jesus's teaching. This second ministry included concepts such as light, love, and new life. But we can't ignore the *first*, and equally important, focus of his teaching: to enlighten everyone around him concerning the true spirit of the law.

> Jesus's *death*, not his birth, is what really initiated the New Testament era.

Here are some excerpts from a killer sermon (Matt. 5:21–48) Jesus delivered as everyone's jaws dropped:

You have heard that it was said to the people long ago, "Do not murder, and anyone who murders will be subject to judgment." *But I tell you* that anyone who is angry with his brother will be subject to *judgment*. (Matt. 5:21–22)

You have heard that it was said, "Do not commit adultery." *But I tell you* that anyone who looks at a woman lustfully has already committed adultery with her in his heart. (Matt. 5:27–28)

If your right eye causes you to sin, gouge it out and throw it away. It is better for you to lose one part of your body than for your whole body *to be thrown into hell*. (Matt. 5:29)

And if your right hand causes you to sin, cut it off and throw it away. It is better for you to lose one part of your body than for *your whole body to go into hell*. (Matt. 5:30)

You have heard that it was said, "Love your neighbor and hate your enemy." *But I tell you:* Love your enemies and pray for those who persecute you, *that you may be sons of your Father in heaven*. (Matt. 5:43–45)

Be perfect, therefore, *as your heavenly Father* is perfect. (Matt. 5:48)

MOSES 2.0

Jesus's listeners were familiar with "Thou shalt not murder" and confident in their ability to keep that commandment. But "Don't even get angry with someone" was certainly a new one they had broken as recently as that morning. Similarly, they'd heard "Thou shalt not commit adultery" and were likely able to resist that temptation. But "Don't even look at a woman with lust"? "How are we supposed to control a split-second impulse?" they might wonder. Then Jesus really drives his point home—he tells them to pluck out their eyes, cut off their hands, and be perfect just like God.

Notice that Jesus refers to Moses several times and then raises the standard. He makes it impossible for anyone to comply. Second, notice the consequences for disobeying his teaching—*judgment* and *being thrown into hell*.

Some have explained Matthew 5 as a passage on spiritual growth applicable to Christians. Based on the consequences threatened by Jesus, I don't believe Jesus is suggesting a path to spiritual growth. Instead, our final destination is in question. It's about whether we'll be "sons of [our] Father in heaven" (5:45) or whether we'll be "thrown into hell" (5:29). That's the context, and those are Jesus's words.

The only reason we survive this "killer" sermon without factoring in the great divide of the cross is that most of us haven't given Jesus's teachings our best effort. With the mentality of "he didn't really mean it," we settle for our own watered-down version of Jesus's teaching. As a consequence, Jesus is no longer a stumbling block. He's only a small bump in the road as we travel toward our goal of "self-improvement."

But now that we've seen the *dividing line* of the cross, we don't have to water down Jesus's harsh teachings. Instead, we can put them in context. Take some time to go back and read through the four Gospels. Notice the *two* ministries of Jesus—his second ministry bringing in the new covenant *but also* his first ministry to condemn the proud with the unattainable, true spirit of the law. This first ministry doesn't showcase your friendly, neighborhood Jesus. This is the Lord with a sword. Jesus repeatedly refers to the law of Moses and then raises the bar.

Introducing Moses 2.0.

What was Jesus's motivation in presenting these impossible teachings? Jesus amplified the law to show that it couldn't possibly be obeyed. He told some to sever body parts. He told others to sell everything they owned. And he even called some "snakes."

What was the result? The rich man went away sad. The Pharisees went away mad. Mission accomplished.

Vancouver 2010

Olympic standards are high. In 2010, the Winter Olympic Games were held in Vancouver, British Columbia. At that time, the ski conditions were such that the downhill slalom competitors were reaching speeds in excess of 90 miles per hour during their practice runs. The average for competitive skiing at this level is usually only in the 85 miles per hour range. So the Olympic Committee decided to start the skiers *lower* on the mountain to prevent them from reaching unmanageable speeds.

The rich man went away sad. The Pharisees went away mad. Mission accomplished.

As we saw in Matthew 5, Jesus invites his listeners to a spiritual Olympics of sorts. But in contrast to the Vancouver Olympic Committee, Jesus takes the starting line and places it *higher* on the mountain. That way, every skier finds it impossible to navigate the course. No one will *ever* make it down, much less earn a medal.

But in a surprising twist, Jesus climbs the mountain himself. Then he skis down in perfect form, earns the gold medal, sets an Olympic record, and hands the medal to us.

Then he shouts to all Olympians, "Danger: Stay off that mountain! Any attempt to ski it will surely result in death."

Now, that mountain won't disappear until heaven and earth disappear with it (Matt. 5:18). And we should respect the mountain (Rom. 7:12). We should gaze up at its peak in admiration. But we have no business trying to survive its treacherous slopes:

> One covenant is *from Mount Sinai* and bears children who are to be *slaves*. . . . But the Jerusalem that is above is free, and she is our mother. (Gal. 4:24, 26)

10

I recently watched a 3-D film on the big screen. Sure, you pay a little extra and you have to wear those glasses. But the experience is definitely worth it. When you enter the theater and the film starts rolling, you get curious. You know, curious about what everything looks like without the glasses. So I started lifting and lowering my glasses to compare the scenery with and without the techy shades.

What's it like without the glasses? Well, let me tell you—it's not pretty. When you remove the 3-D glasses, you end up seeing the same film but with blurred lines. Nothing lines up correctly, and you don't get that high-resolution, in-your-face experience. But once you put the glasses back on, there it is again. Same film, same theater, but the glasses change everything.

That's exactly what it's like to read your Bible without a new covenant lens. Things just don't line up quite right. Yeah, we might understand the basic gospel message, but things still remain blurry. Once we see Jesus's death as the dividing line of human history, we begin to place the teaching and events in the Bible in proper context. We begin to see the gospel for what it really is—a beautiful, high-resolution, in-your-face experience of God's grace.

The cross provides a whole new perspective on the law of Moses and on Jesus's harsh teachings, Moses 2.0. But if we don't see Jesus's death as the dividing line of human history, we're left with two options for interpreting his difficult teachings—either we interpret them as literal and for us today, or we relegate them to the realm of hyperbole and seek to obey some lesser, more palatable version of his teaching.

Let's examine those options.

Option 1: The Literal, Applicable Approach

First, if Jesus's harsh teachings are to be taken literally and as applicable for us today, then there should be a lot of amputees in our churches. I don't mean to be flippant, but that *is* the literal interpretation of his words. Jesus also literally said that we should try to be perfect just like God, that we should sell all of our belongings and give to the poor, and that (as it says in the Lord's Prayer) we will only receive the same quantity and quality of forgiveness from God that we have first doled out to others (see Matt. 6:12, 14–15).

Ouch! If we are to apply these harsh teachings to our lives today, we quickly arrive at a couple of depressing conclusions. First, there are no Christians living this out! Second, we're all doomed to be "thrown into hell" (Matt.

5:22, 29–30) since we're not "sons of the Father in heaven" (Matt. 5:45). In addition, if we take Jesus's harsh teachings as literal, then Matthew 5 becomes a works salvation passage. After all, salvation itself—heaven or hell—is clearly on the line (Matt. 5:22, 30).

OPTION 2: THE HYPERBOLE APPROACH

Some have tried to explain the stringency of Jesus's harsh teachings by claiming that they are hyperbole (exaggeration). "Jesus just meant for us to do our best, with his help," they might say.

Again, consider what's on the line in this teaching—if you don't live up to these commands, you will encounter "judgment" and be "thrown into hell" (Matt. 5:20–22, 29–30). If you don't love your enemies, you aren't even given the right to be "sons of your Father in heaven" (Matt. 5:45). So if we decide that Jesus didn't really mean what he said about meeting this higher standard of the law, then was Jesus also "exaggerating" about the *consequences* of disobedience—judgment and being thrown into hell?

There are no Christians living this out!

Personally, I'm uncomfortable recasting the words of Jesus as exaggeration to make his teachings more palatable. His harsh teachings don't appear to be mere suggestions for a bit of holy living. This is life and death. If you're going to attempt to live by the teachings of Jesus in Matthew 5, you'd better have more willpower than anyone in human history! But the reality is that most of us Christians have chosen to retain our limbs, our eyes, and our possessions.

We also admit that we're not perfectly behaved like our heavenly Father. Every day, our lives prove that Jesus's harsh teachings are impossible on any practical level.

It's easy to see why Jesus-as-hyperbole is a popular interpretation. To the verses about severing body parts and selling everything, we might say, "He just meant that we should take sin seriously. And he didn't literally mean to sell everything. He just meant that we shouldn't love money." Fair enough. But consider how Jesus's audience of that day responded to his harsh teachings: by being confused and discouraged (Mark 10:22). Whatever our interpretation today, there's no doubt that Jesus's listeners believed he meant those statements *literally*.

OPTION 3: *WEARING THE GLASSES*

Maybe you're not comfortable saying Jesus's harsh teachings are to be taken literally and are applicable to us today. But maybe you don't like the idea of watering them down as hyperbole either. Well, there is a third option. Here it is: we can interpret Jesus's teachings as literal but contextualize them as being *directed at people who were still under the law* (Gal. 4:4–5).

Are you looking through *new* *covenant* glasses?

The only interpretation that seems to make sense is that Jesus meant what he said, literally and actually. However, there's a historical setting, a spiritual context, and an audience to factor in when we read Jesus's radical statements.

Remember my experience watching the 3-D movie *without* my glasses on? Things were pretty blurry. Similarly, have you been trying to make sense of Jesus's harsh teachings without a clear understanding of the dividing line of the cross? In other words, are you looking at Scripture, life, and your relationship with God through *new covenant* glasses?

If not, everything will remain fuzzy.

AN ANCIENT INFOMERCIAL

Sometimes I'll be flipping through the channels late at night and land on one of those mesmerizing infomercials. What impresses me the most is the "before and after" pictures they show you. The person on the left always looks so depressed. Then in the photo on the right, the same person looks amazingly different! (Sometimes I wonder if they literally use *someone else's* picture as the "after" photo.)

Which person would you rather be like? The "after" person, of course! That's their sales pitch: if you feel like "before," sad and out of shape, just send in a check for $19.95 plus shipping and handling, and we'll turn *you* into that "after" picture.

That's exactly what God offers, but without the spin. In contrast to infomercial products, God's new way is 100 percent guaranteed to turn us into a different person. Not only that, it's free of charge—or at least someone else paid for it.

Just like those infomercials, Jesus and the authors of the New Testament paint a compelling "before and after" picture for us. First, they show how hopeless things were "before," under the law. And boy, was it an ugly picture—exhaustion and a crippling sense of failure. But then they paint a vivid picture of the "after" life. Under God's new way, we obtain a closeness with God those under the old only dreamed of. We're born a second time (John 3:3–7) with a new human spirit and God's Spirit living in us (Ezek. 36:26–27). We belong to God no matter what (2 Tim. 2:13; 1 Pet. 2:9). And while the old way left Israel torn and tattered in their attempts to obey, the new way causes us to want what God wants (Phil. 2:13; Heb. 8:10).

Through this new way, God fixed every problem we had under the law. As a free gift, he makes us right forever (2 Cor. 5:21); he redesigns us as an expression of his very nature (2 Pet. 1:4); and he forgives us completely and unconditionally (Heb. 10:14). When we enter into relationship with God through the new covenant, things change forever (Heb. 7:12). We "serve in the new way of the Spirit, and not in the old way of the written code" (Rom. 7:6). We serve God, *without* religion.

THE SECOND MINISTRY OF CHRIST

As we've seen, Jesus brought *two* ministries with him to planet earth. First, Jesus buried his Jewish contemporaries under the true demands of the *old* covenant. Second, he prophesied about a *new* covenant to come. But this new covenant ministry involves a hope that we still haven't touched on. Through Jesus's second ministry, he introduced a new hope to those of us *outside the Jewish world.*

But who among us can enjoy this new covenant—anyone in the whole world? Or is this new hope limited to individuals whom God has already preselected?

The old covenant was limited to a select group—the Jews. Your eligibility for the old way of the law was pre-determined by your birth. You were either in Club Israel, or you weren't. But this changed under the new covenant. The wall between Jews and Gentiles was demolished (Eph. 2:14). The Son of Man was lifted up, and he began to draw *all* men to himself (John 12:32).

So let's take a closer look at Christ's second ministry—his new covenant move to include non-Jews in the gospel. As we do, you'll be invited to jettison what I call "Grade A *Choice* Religion."

PART 4

GOD'S BIG FAT GREEK WEDDING

What shall we say then? That Gentiles, who did not pursue righteousness, attained righteousness.

the apostle Paul (Rom. 9:30 NASB)

11

Fate or free will? Plato or Socrates? Calvin or Arminius? For thousands of years, we've been asking, "Is everything fated, or is there free will? Is our every move preplanned by an outside force, or do we have freedom to move about the planet as we please?"

What a headache! And apparently, what a way to divide churches! Predestination—the idea that God appointed some to salvation and left others for eternal damnation—has spawned church divisions all over the world. Believers in predestination, free will, and hybrid versions of each split philosophical hairs as they debate one of the most controversial subjects in the Christian faith, often using complicated terminology and even cryptic jargon.

Was this what the apostle Paul intended for the church when he penned the word *predestined* a mere four times in only two of his letters? Would he want us to replay the Plato-Socrates fate debate, over and over, with a Jesus stamp on it? With the first traces of the church debate over fate versus free will coming on the scene *hundreds of years after the cross*, one has to wonder how the first-century church viewed the idea of "individual selection" by God, if they contemplated it at all.

POPULAR POSITIONS

"Romans and Ephesians clearly say that God predestined us! How can you say he didn't?" one says.

"But Romans talks about the importance of calling on the name of Jesus, and that's a choice *we* make. We're not robots!" someone else replies.

Then the peacemaker chimes in, "Look, you're both right. God chose us *and* we chose him. They're both true. We just can't understand it this side of heaven."

If you've been in a church long enough, you've likely heard one or more of these three ideas: (1) God chose us to be saved; (2) we chose God out of our own free will; or (3) God chose us *and* we chose God, but we just can't understand it.

Of course, there are different flavors of these. But to get the gist, we need only concern ourselves with the two extremes and what I call the "intellectual gymnastics view"—that they're somehow *both* right.

For all of the trouble predestination has caused, it's amazing that the term appears only four times in the entire Bible! It's obvious that certain acts of God were preplanned ahead of time so they would happen at a future date. But the question here is: Under the new covenant, *who* is predestined?

THE NIGERIAN LETTER

The press recently reported on John Worley, a Christian psychotherapist who was perusing his email inbox one day when he noticed a message from someone with an African name. Worley opened the email to find a rather lengthy message containing a request for assistance in wire transferring some money. After brief consideration, Worley wrote back, "I can help, and I am interested."

> Under the new covenant, *who* is predestined?

Worley attributed his lucky opportunity to "God's will." And he fell for the idea of advancing a large sum of money to the African business-man in hopes that he would receive a promised sixteen million dollars in return.

Needless to say, things didn't work out the way Worley had planned.

Maybe you've received an email like the one Worley did. I get one nearly every day. This Nigerian letter is a multi-billion-dollar scam that began decades before the advent of email. The selling point is that for simply sending some money in advance, you are promised a much larger sum in return.

What's the first mistake victims make? Perhaps it's assuming that the email was sent to them *exclusively*. They think they've been singled out. If they were told that thousands had received the same email, they might not be so quick to be scammed. If we don't know any different, it's only natural for us to assume that an email like the one Worley received is the result of someone singling us out. We want to believe that we're the lucky one, that we individually hit the jackpot. It's this type of thinking that opens us up to errors in judgment, wrong conclusions, and poor choices.

As we'll see, it's not much different when it comes to Paul's letters and predestination. In Ephesians, for example, we read the word *you* and might assume that it means us, *individually*. And with that idea as our starting point, it only naturally follows that God engaged in individual selection by choosing each of us for heaven and leaving others hopeless.

What if "you" is plural and doesn't mean individuals were picked?

But what if the truth of the gospel is simpler than that? What if "you" is plural and doesn't mean individuals were picked while others were left for eternal damnation? And what if it takes no mental gymnastics at all to fit the pieces together? With so many thousands of pages written on the predestination puzzle, could it really be *simple*?

A Tale of Two Teams

Paul's letter to the Ephesians opens with God choosing someone for adoption, and the term "us" is used:

> For *he chose us* in him before the creation of the world to be holy and blameless in his sight. In love *he predestined us* to be adopted as his sons through Jesus Christ. (Eph. 1:4–5)

A popular interpretation is that Paul is referring to "us Christians," saying that God chose us Christians and predestined us Christians for sonship. But I wonder if that's the best reading of the passage. Of course, Christians are holy, blameless, and adopted. But it seems that the "us" in this passage is a bit more *specific* than just "us Christians." Let's see if we can figure out what Paul really means:

> In him *we were also chosen, having been predestined* according to the plan of him who works out everything in conformity with the purpose of his will, in order that *we, who were the first to hope in Christ*, might be for the praise of his glory. (Eph. 1:11–12)

Again we see the words *chosen* and *predestined* describing a group called "we." The "we" here refers to the *first* people to put their hope in Christ. Of course, the first people would be the apostles themselves and their fellow *Jews*. They believed first.

Then things get really interesting. Paul mentions a second group of people. He directly addresses this second group by saying:

> And *you also* were included in Christ when you heard the word of truth, the gospel of your salvation. (Eph. 1:13)

Of course, by "you also," Paul means his audience—the Ephesians, who are *Gentiles*. As we read on, we see Paul contrast the two groups again:

> As for *you*, you were dead in your transgressions and sins. . . . *All of us also* lived among them at one time, gratifying the cravings of our sinful nature and following its desires and thoughts. *Like the rest, we* were by nature deserving of wrath. (Eph. 2:1, 3)

Paul says the Ephesians were dead in their sins. Then he says "all of *us also*." So what's this all about? Why does Paul refer to a group called "we" that includes himself and then to another group called "you"? This is an important question as we look at the true, contextualized meaning of predestination.

As we'll see, the most straightforward reading of these chapters in Ephesians is the following: Paul refers many times to himself, the apostles, and his fellow Jews by using "we" and "us." And he refers to the Ephesians (Gentiles) by using "you" and, in particular, "you *also*."

AN ANCIENT "Y'ALL"

This all sounds great, but does the grammar support this interpretation? Yes, the grammar supports it. Since the letter was addressed to hundreds or even thousands of Ephesians, the *you* here (the Greek plural pronoun *humeis*) is a *plural* you. It's like a southern "y'all," as we say here in Texas. As we read on in Ephesians, this "you plural" only becomes clearer:

> Therefore, remember that formerly *you who are Gentiles by birth* and called "uncircumcised" by those who call themselves "the circumcision" (that done in the body by the hands of men)—remember that at that time *you were separate from Christ*, excluded from citizenship in Israel and foreigners to the covenants of the promise, without hope and without God in the world. But now in Christ Jesus *you who once were far away* have been brought near through the blood of Christ. (Eph. 2:11–13)

Our first inclination might be to read a verse that says "you" as referring to ourselves, individually. But that's not the context here. In this passage, "you" is clearly and unmistakably plural, referring to the Ephesians—all of whom were Gentiles. Paul goes on to call them "uncircumcised" (v. 11), "excluded from citizenship" (v. 12), and "far away" (v. 13). Clearly, Paul is addressing them *as Gentiles*.

THE RACE CARD

So why does Paul play the race card here? Remember that Gentiles were seen as unclean and unworthy to commune with God. The Jews looked at Gentiles as the lowest form of humanity on earth. The Gentiles had no hope, no calling, no covenant, and no relationship with the one and only God.

> **What does this mean for our modern-day debate over predestination of *individuals?***

In historical context, Paul's words are highly controversial! How could Paul, who himself was a Jew and a Pharisee, be so bold as to claim that the dirty Gentiles had been brought near to God? But this is precisely Paul's claim:

> For he himself is our peace, who has *made the two one* and has destroyed the barrier. . . . His purpose was to create in himself *one new humanity out of the two*, thus making peace, and in one body *to reconcile both of them* to God through the cross. (Eph. 2:14–16)

If context reveals that God's predestined plan was to bring the gospel to *Gentiles*, what does this mean for our modern-day debate over predestination of *individuals?*

That's a question we'll save for a little bit later. First, we'd better be certain that is what's really going on here. If we are genuinely going to experience God *without* religion (even Grade A Choice Religion!), we can't leave any stone unturned.

12

My *Big Fat Greek Wedding* is a film about thirtysome-thing Toula Portokalos, who lives in a Greek com-munity in Chicago. Toula works in her father's Greek restaurant, Dancing Zorba's. Toula's father wants her to marry a nice Greek man, have lots of Greek children, and settle down to a traditional Greek life. But Toula is search-ing for more in life and finds it when she meets Ian Miller. Ian is a high school English teacher who is *not* Greek by any stretch. After hiding their relationship as long as they can, the cat is eventually let out of the bag, and Toula's dad blows his stack.

If you've seen this movie, you know that the humor revolves around two *very* different families. Ian Miller comes from an unexpressive, sterile American family. In contrast, Toula knows only the chatty, in-your-face Greek life. Throughout the movie, Ian's parents are continually alarmed by the Greeks—a fire pit in the front yard complete with roasted pig, an aunt who tells them stomach-churning stories about a tumor twin, and strong liquors that send the Millers' heads spinning.

The Millers see Toula's Greek family as brash, uncultured, and perhaps even "unclean." Although the movie exaggerates with stereotypes, the plot certainly wasn't birthed out of thin air. The fact is that historically, some have looked upon Greeks as precisely that—unclean.

Specifically, the *Jewish* perspective on Greeks is important to grasp when it comes to interpreting large portions of the New Testament. In fact, one of the most controversial Christian beliefs of our time (predestination) cannot be properly understood without realizing how Jews looked at Greeks.

> Predestination is about "God's Big Fat Greek Wedding."

As we put predestination in its scriptural context, a startling simplicity will be revealed.

Here's what we'll find: predestination is about "God's Big Fat Greek Wedding" as he controversially opened up his gospel message to a new bride, the Greeks. *It was never intended to be about individual selection of some for heaven while leaving others for hell.*

Just as the Miller family was skeptical of their son's unorthodox union with Toula, the Jews were skeptical of Yahweh joining himself to "those dirty Gentiles." For that reason, the apostle Paul went to great lengths to defend God's sovereign choice *to save Gentiles*.

So if Jesus's second ministry (through the *new* covenant) involved offering the gospel to *all* Gentile nations, then predestination is *not* about God preselecting some individuals and leaving others for hell.

GOD'S BIG FAT GREEK WEDDING

God's predestined plan through the cross was to demolish any spiritual difference between Jews and Gentiles. By making the law irrelevant to new life in Christ, he made the two groups one. With God's plan in mind, Paul gives another clarification about the "you" he is writing to:

> He came and preached peace to *you who were far away* and peace to *those who were near*. For through him *we both* have access to the Father by one Spirit. (Eph. 2:17–18)

Notice that "you" is defined as "you who were far away" (v. 17). Again, Paul means Gentiles here. When he says "those who were near" (v. 17), he means Jews. Then he lumps them both together, saying "we both" (v. 18).

The Jewish people carried the same bloodline as the prophets. They had a heritage full of covenant, promise, and God's faithfulness. They were already *near*—near to the gospel message. It was first announced from the lips of Israel's prophets and then heard through Jewish apostles. Nevertheless, Paul stresses that "we both" (Jews and Gentiles) now have access to God by the same Spirit. The result of this access is described this way:

> Consequently, *you are no longer foreigners and aliens*, but fellow citizens with God's people. . . . And in him *you too* are being built together to become a dwelling in which God lives by his Spirit. (Eph. 2:19, 22)

Gentiles were *foreigners* and *strangers* when it came to the things of God. But now Paul says Gentiles "are being built together" (v. 22). Notice again that he says "you *too*" here, meaning "you Gentiles also, not just us Jews." Then, as Paul's third chapter opens, we see him once again revealing what "you" means:

> For this reason I, Paul, the prisoner of Christ Jesus for the sake of *you Gentiles*. (Eph. 3:1)

A MYSTERY MADE PLAIN

Maybe you're still unsure about the true meaning of predestination in Ephesians. Here's how Paul concludes everything he wrote them about it. Here we see talk of an ancient (preplanned) mystery that has now been revealed. You can decide for yourself *whom* you think was predestined and *to what*:

> The mystery of Christ, which was *not made known to men in other generations* as it has now been revealed by the Spirit to God's holy apostles and prophets. *This mystery is that through the gospel the Gentiles are heirs together with Israel*, members together of one body, and sharers together in the promise in Christ Jesus. . . . and *to make plain to everyone* the administration of this mystery, which *for ages past was kept hidden* in God, who created all things. (Eph. 3:4–6, 9)

God's plan was predestined a long time ago. It was not made known for generations. It was kept hidden. But now, through the new covenant inaugurated in Jesus's death, it's been revealed. Here Paul tells us *exactly* what it is! He says it's that "through the gospel *the Gentiles* are heirs together with Israel" (v. 4). So are you still in doubt about what was predestined by God and is now revealed? Apparently, Paul thinks he's made it "plain to everyone" (v. 9).

Well, that's it. That's every verse related to predestination in all of Ephesians. And Ephesians is one of only two epistles that even use the term "predestined." So if you're now considering the idea that predestination in Ephesians might be about God's selection of the Gentiles, then guess what? There's only one more place to go—Romans—before we've looked at every major passage about this controversial issue.

THE GENTILE APPOINTMENT

Understanding the Jewish-Gentile context for predestination doesn't just help with Ephesians and Romans. It also helps us understand the corporate (collective) nature of every verse that speaks of God's "chosen" people or the "elect." In the Old Testament, God's chosen people meant Israel, collectively. In the New Testament, God's chosen people (or the elect) also refers to a collective group—the church.

Realizing that God appointed Gentiles to salvation also helps us understand one of the most debated stand-alone passages of all:

> Then Paul and Barnabas answered them boldly: "We had to speak the word of God *to you first*. Since you reject it and do not consider yourselves worthy of eternal life, *we now turn to the Gentiles*. For this is what the Lord has commanded us: 'I have made you a light *for the Gentiles*, that you may bring salvation to the ends of the earth.' When

the Gentiles heard this, they were glad and honored the word of the Lord; and *all who were appointed for eternal life believed*. (Acts 13:46–48)

The last phrase in this passage—"all who were appointed for eternal life believed" (v. 48)—has been taken out of context by many to support the idea of individual selection. But the emphasis here is on them *being Gentiles*. Yes, as many as were present and heard the gospel believed. But in historical context, the major news flash was that "those dirty Gentiles" (as a whole, including those present for this event) had been appointed to life!

You might be thinking, "Okay, I get it. Predestination is about God's controversial choice to include the Gentiles in the gospel. But isn't individual selection clearly taught in Romans?" Good question, and that's where we're headed next. But before we go there, consider this: The belief in individual selection has been built primarily on Ephesians and Romans. So what if both of these Epistles prove to mean something different? Besides some stray verses about God's "chosen" people or the "elect" (referring to the church collectively), is there anything left in the Bible on which to build a claim that Jesus's new covenant offer isn't open to *everyone*?

13

The first mention of predestination in Romans is in the eighth chapter:

> And we know that in all things God works for the good of those who love him, who have been called according to his purpose. For those God foreknew he also predestined *to be conformed to the image of his Son*, that he might be the firstborn among many brothers and sisters. And those he predestined, he also called; those he called, he also justified; those he justified, he also glorified. (Rom. 8:28–30)

God knows the future. He foreknew who among us would come to salvation. But knowing the future doesn't mean controlling our choices. Here we need to read carefully and ask: predestined to *what*? There's a clear answer: predestined to be conformed to Christ's image. *This is referring to our spiritual growth.* We are being conformed to Christ's image because God looked at all his children down the timeline of human history and promised in advance that he would work all things together for our growth.

So Paul is *not* talking about the selection of Gentiles for the gospel just yet. Instead, he's talking about what Christians *corporately* are predestined for. As the church, we are designed by God to be conformed to Christ's image, to have a heavenly calling, to be right (justified) before God, and to one day see God face-to-face in our glorified state. This passage is akin to saying "He who began a good work in you will carry it on to completion" (Phil. 1:6). All Christians are *collectively* predestined to become conformed to Christ's image over time. Here Paul is saying our growth in Christ is a sure thing!

This was encouraging for the Romans to read, since they were suffering (v. 18) and experiencing weakness (v. 26).

Our growth in Christ is a sure thing!

Paul wanted them to know that God was for them (v. 31) and that God had their maturity in mind. God was working in the midst of their suffering to conform them to his image. So there was purpose in their suffering. That's the context of this passage.

These three verses (vv. 28–30) were never intended to stand alone to form a doctrine of individual selection. They should be understood in context as encouragement for those suffering. That's what is expressed in the chapter as a whole.

It's also true that we Christians are *collectively* "chosen" (v. 33), just as Israel was collectively God's chosen people. But what are we chosen *for*? Again, in context, we are chosen for conformity to Christ's image, to have a heavenly calling, for closeness to God, and for a future glory. This is what God has chosen for all Christians, collectively. This is very different from saying that God chose one individual for heaven and left another for hell. *If Paul had wanted to communicate individual selection in this passage, he certainly could have done so very clearly.* The straightforward reading here is that the heavenly calling (purpose) and predestined conformity (growth) of the Romans was communicated as encouragement to them in the midst of their "trouble" and "hardship" (v. 35).

THE DONALD TRUMP

The name Donald Trump is synonymous with success. Trump demands excellence, whether it's in real estate investment, sports, or entertainment. His high standards and his ability to make things happen are the basis for the popular TV show *The Apprentice*. On the show, contestants are subjected to tough business challenges and close scrutiny as Trump sets everything up and judges the outcomes. And every show ends with Trump's famous line, "You're fired!"

> God is playing his trump card.

Say what you will about Donald Trump, there's one thing we know for sure—*he* calls the shots. Whether it's who's being hired or who's being fired, whatever he says goes. Nobody argues with *the* Donald Trump.

Nobody.

In Ephesians (and, as we'll see, in Romans), God is playing his trump (or Trump, if you will) card. He's saying, "I call the shots!" Paul makes that point over and over as he shows God's history of doing whatever he wants—with Jacob, Esau, Pharaoh, and so many more. Whatever the case, God always gets it done, his way.

Our job is to respect him. We may not understand what he's up to or even agree with it! Still, we're called to revere his sovereignty. But here's the catch: Paul introduces us to the sovereignty of God *not* to justify *individual* selection of Christians. As we read through Ephesians and Romans, we find that God played his trump card a *different* way. He played it in the selection of "those dirty Gentiles" to inherit the gospel.

Two thousand years ago, that didn't sit well with the establishment.

GOD'S TRUMP CARD

Romans is strikingly similar to Ephesians. Both epistles include a predestination discussion that is *absolutely surrounded by verbiage about Jews and Gentiles.* Here Paul launches into a Jew-versus-Gentile discussion just as he did in Ephesians, speaking of "the people of Israel":

> Theirs is the adoption as sons; theirs the divine glory, the covenants, the receiving of the law, the temple worship and the promises. (Rom. 9:4)

Paul first notes that Israel *deserves* the gospel in some sense—even Jesus himself came through a Jewish bloodline. But then Paul says something to justify the inclusion of Gentiles:

> It is not the natural children who are God's children, but
> it is the children of the promise who are regarded as Abra-
> ham's offspring. (Rom. 9:8)

So who would be the natural children? Each and every
Jew. But who in fact are the children of the promise? Anyone, Jew or Gentile, who puts their faith in Jesus Christ. *So
what is all this talk of Jew and Gentile doing in the middle
of a passage that is supposedly about individual selection?*

Paul is saying that God can do whatever he wants. In his
divine wisdom, he chose to include the Gentiles and elect
them for salvation as well. This was controversial, since
the average Jew thought a Gentile had no business even
dreaming of knowing God.

GOD'S RIGHT TO CHOOSE

Next is Paul's Old Testament reference to Rebecca's twins,
which he uses as an example to argue that God has always
done as he pleases:

> Yet, before the twins were born or had done anything good
> or bad—*in order that God's purpose in election might
> stand*: not by works but by him who calls—she was told,
> "The older will serve the younger." Just as it is written:
> "Jacob I loved, but Esau I hated." (Rom. 9:11–13)

God loved Jacob and hated Esau. And God chose to do
this before either of them was born. There is no question
about that. The real question is *why Paul is bringing this
up.* Is it to justify the idea that God handpicks Christians
today for heaven and leaves others for hell?

Interestingly, Paul doesn't go there. Paul's point has nothing to do with individual selection on this side of the cross. Now, I can understand how someone might conclude such a thing. We pick up the Bible and read it and we naturally make it about us, as individuals. But notice how Paul connects the dots for us *New* Testament saints. Interestingly, he transitions into a discussion of *how God made a radical move to include Gentiles in the gospel*, not just Jews:

> What if God, choosing to show his wrath and make his power known, bore with great patience *the objects of his wrath*—prepared for destruction? What if he did this to make the riches of his glory known to *the objects of his mercy*, whom he prepared in advance for glory—even us, whom he also called, *not only from the Jews but also from the Gentiles*? (Rom. 9:22–24)

Who were the objects of God's wrath? Gentiles. And what is this passage about? It's about God's plan to show off his patience as he saves people, not just from the Jews but also from the Gentiles. On this side of the cross, *either Jew or Gentile* can receive a heavenly calling in Christ Jesus!

GOD'S CIVIL RIGHTS MOVEMENT

In the late 1800s, laws in the South resulted in the separation of blacks and whites in the United States. African Americans were considered second-class citizens, while whites were wrongly regarded as superior. In many cases, African Americans were required to use separate schools, restaurants, bus and train seating, telephone booths, and toilets. State laws also prevented interracial marriages and restricted the voting rights of African Americans.

But all of this would soon change.

On July 26, 1948, President Harry Truman signed an executive order that stated, "There shall be equality of treatment and opportunity for all persons in the armed services without regard to race, color, religion, or national origin." From there the civil rights movement, aimed at outlawing racial discrimination, began to transform American society. Schools that were previously segregated opened up to African American students. Buses and restaurants stopped their racial segregation. Slowly, the mentality all over the United States, especially in the South, changed. People began to see African Americans in a new and proper light.

> Racism is not something we like to think about when reading the Bible.

BIGOTRY IN THE BIBLE

Racism is not something we like to think about when reading the Bible. But racism is precisely what was occurring two thousand years ago between Jews and Gentiles. And it wasn't just an attitude. There was segregation, just as we witnessed here in the United States:

> When Peter came to Antioch, I opposed him to his face, because he was clearly in the wrong. Before certain men came from James, *he used to eat with the Gentiles*. But when they arrived, he began to draw back and *separate himself from the Gentiles* because he was afraid of those

who belonged to the circumcision group. The *other Jews joined him* in his hypocrisy, so that by their hypocrisy even Barnabas was led astray. (Gal. 2:11–13)

Racism, plain and simple. And we need to factor in this racism when we read the Bible. Then we understand why Paul had to defend his apostleship to the Gentiles.

If you've wondered why Paul goes on for nearly three chapters in Romans about God's choice, *this* is why. He was defending God's most radical decision ever: the unleashing of the gospel on "dirty Gentiles." Sure, this predestined plan had been promised to Abraham—that he'd be the father of *many* nations. But actually carrying out that plan? Now that's offensive!

The controversy wasn't about God picking one person here and another person there. *God had already been doing that throughout the Old Testament!* That was old news, as God had chosen Jacob, Moses, David, and others for divine acts of service. The big news flash in Paul's day was that God was calling an entire people group who were historically *not* his people. Given the thousands of years that God had reserved himself for Israel, it was definitely an offense to the Jewish ego!

"But the ninth chapter of Romans is famous for support- ing God's *individual* selection of us! The analogy about God being the potter and us being the clay must mean he chose us individually. How can you say it's all about God's selection of *Gentiles*?" some will ask. Clearly, the only way to get to the bottom of this is to continue reading in context. So let's do it!

14

Paul draws two parallels related to God's choice concerning Gentiles. First, he compares this new covenant decision with God's right to harden Pharaoh's heart in the Old Testament. Then Paul compares this new covenant decision with a potter who can do whatever he wants with his clay:

> For He says to Moses, "I WILL HAVE MERCY ON WHOM I HAVE MERCY, AND I WILL HAVE COMPASSION ON WHOM I HAVE COMPASSION." *So then it does not depend on the man who wills or the man who runs, but on God who has mercy.* For the Scripture says to Pharaoh, "FOR THIS VERY PURPOSE I RAISED YOU UP, TO DEMONSTRATE MY POWER IN YOU, AND THAT MY NAME MIGHT BE PROCLAIMED *THROUGHOUT THE WHOLE EARTH*." So then He has mercy on whom He desires, and He hardens whom He desires. You will say to me then, "Why does He still find fault? For who resists His will?" On the contrary, who are you, O man, who answers back to God? The thing molded will not say to the molder, "Why did you make me like this," will it? *Or does not the*

potter have a right over the clay, to make from the same lump one vessel for honorable use and another for common use? (Rom. 9:15–21 NASB)

God can have mercy on whomever he wants. In the Old Testament, he even *hardened* whomever he wanted! Pharaoh is a perfect example. God exercised his right to harden Pharaoh's heart so that God's name "might be proclaimed throughout the whole earth" (Rom. 9:17). So why is God showing mercy to Gentiles? For the same reason—to proclaim his name throughout the *whole* earth, not just among Jews!

Notice that it doesn't depend on the man who wills or runs. It's not about human effort but about God who has mercy. To some, this might sound like an argument for individual selection. But Paul explains his meaning just a few verses later when he says, "What shall we say then? That *Gentiles, who did not pursue righteousness*, attained righteousness, even the righteousness which is by faith; but *Israel, pursuing* a law of righteousness, did not arrive at that law" (Rom. 9:30–31 NASB).

This is *not* about individual selection.

Who was the man who was running and pursuing? The Jew. And who was the man who was shown mercy? The Gentile. The Gentiles were not running after righteousness. They didn't care about God in the least! Still, God chose them for the gospel.

This is *not* about individual selection. Paul is defending God's sovereign choice to have mercy on a group that wasn't even pursuing righteousness—the Gentiles.

THE PURPOSE OF THE POTTER

Paul gives the potter analogy to emphasize God's right to choose. Of course, some think this analogy relates to heaven and hell for individuals. But if a piece of clay is for "common use," that's hardly an analogy for hell. A better analogy for hell would be disposing of the clay altogether, not giving it a common use!

No, the main point here is that God is a potter who can do whatever he wants with his own craft. In context, the Master Potter's right to choose was exercised when he extended the gospel to the Gentile nations through Jesus. The verses that immediately follow the potter analogy make this very clear:

> *What if God*, choosing to show his wrath and make his power known, *bore with great patience the objects of his wrath*—prepared for destruction? What if he did this *to make the riches of his glory known* to the objects of his mercy, whom he prepared in advance for glory—even us, whom he also called, *not only from the Jews but also from the Gentiles*? (Rom. 9:22–24)

God endured the Gentiles and their absurdly sinful ways for so long (v. 22). And he endured them so that he could one day prepare them for glory (vv. 23–24). This plan was hidden in the Old Testament. The Jews simply could not see it or bring themselves to believe it. But Paul notes that it's right here in the prophecy of Hosea:

> As he says in Hosea: "*I will call them 'my people' who are not my people*; and I will call her 'my loved one' who is not my loved one," and, "It will happen that in

the very place where it was said to them, 'You are not my people,' they will be called 'sons of the living God.'" (Rom. 9:25–26)

A CLEAR CONCLUSION

So who did not belong to God? Gentiles. And who were not God's "loved one"? Gentiles. We see this line of reasoning in the verses that follow the quote from Hosea:

> What shall we say then? That Gentiles, who did not pursue righteousness, attained righteousness, even the righteousness which is by faith; but Israel, pursuing a law of righteousness, did not arrive at that law." (Rom. 9:30–31 NASB)

"What shall we say then?" is the marker for Paul's *main purpose* in bringing all of this up! We should see this statement as an enormous red flag waving in the air to indicate *why* Paul has been saying all that he has said.

Could it be that the true meaning of predestination is staring us in the face?

MINING AFGHANISTAN

In 2010, media outlets all over the world reported that vast mineral deposits were discovered in Afghanistan. What is currently a war-torn wasteland in many ways now has a second chance.

The discovery of iron, copper, gold, and lithium is projected to turn Afghanistan into a major mining center. In fact, a Pentagon memo states that Afghanistan may soon be known as the "Saudi Arabia of lithium," as the precious mineral is now a hot commodity used in batteries for all kinds of electronics.

Some are now thinking of Afghanistan as a wealthy nation. But weren't they actually wealthy all along? After all, the mineral deposits, and the potential for exploiting them, have *always* been there. One might even say that God had "predestined" Afghanistan to be a world leader in the mining industry. It was just that the potential hadn't been revealed until United States government officials and geologists announced their findings.

This is how predestination is truly compatible with free will.

In Romans, the apostle Paul is making a similar announcement, telling everyone that the gospel has made their lands rich. They are no longer a barren land of Gentiles. They have potential for great wealth in the spiritual realm.

But just as important decisions lie ahead for Afghanistan, Gentiles can squander their opportunity too. Sure, God predestined that we be given the greatest offer of all time. But we must capitalize on that opportunity: "Everyone who *calls on* the name of the Lord will be saved" (Rom. 10:13).

This is how predestination is truly compatible with free will, without any mental gymnastics or the delay of understanding it "later, in heaven." The hidden wealth of the gospel has now been revealed, on Gentile soil. And we *choose* to mine for it and glean from it all the riches that are in Jesus Christ.

The Free Choice

This free choice is exactly why Paul tells the Romans the following:

> "Do not say in your heart, 'Who will ascend into heaven?'" (that is, to bring Christ down) "or 'Who will descend into the deep?'" (that is, to bring Christ up from the dead). (Rom. 10:6–7)

This is precisely what the Jews were saying—that Gentiles couldn't go to heaven. Paul is saying, "Don't try to predict such a thing, especially given that righteousness is now a gift and has nothing to do with the law."

So where is individual selection of some for heaven and others for hell in this passage? It is entirely absent. It's not Paul's point at all. Paul's only message concerning God's selection has to do with people groups, not individuals. It's all about Jews and Gentiles. It's not about you versus the guy next door. Paul says the following, which throws open the door of salvation to anyone:

> That if you confess with your mouth, "Jesus is Lord," and believe in your heart that God raised him from the dead, you will be saved. . . . As the Scripture says, "*Anyone* who trusts in him will never be put to shame." (Rom. 10:9, 11)

Paul says belief in Jesus is essential and will not disappoint. And even now, a full chapter later, he is still harping on the two people groups:

> For there is *no difference between Jew and Gentile*—the same Lord is Lord of all and richly blesses all who call on

him, for, "*Everyone who calls on* the name of the Lord will be saved." (Rom. 10:12–13)

From here, Paul goes on for a full chapter about the importance of personal belief in Jesus Christ. He says "how can they believe in the one of whom they have not heard?" (Rom. 10:14). He says that anyone can be grafted into God's kingdom "if they do not persist in unbelief" (Rom. 11:23). Finally, he says that God has carried out this plan "so that he may have mercy on them all" (Rom. 11:32). Clearly, the message delivered is that "*everyone* who calls on the name of the Lord will be saved" (Rom. 10:13).

> Predestination is about God's plan to unleash the gospel on "those dirty Gentiles."

THE BIG PICTURE

So in both Ephesians and Romans, the big picture presented is this:

- God is God.
- He can do whatever he wants.
- He elected the Gentiles for salvation as well.
- Now anyone can come to Christ by faith.
- Deal with this reality! It's God's sovereign choice.

Predestination is real. It's a biblical term and a biblical concept. But what does it really mean? In context, we've seen that it's about God's plan to unleash the gospel on "those dirty Gentiles." It's not about individual selection.

With God's true intentions in mind, it's our job to revere God's sovereign choice to unleash the gospel on Gentiles (that's most of us!) *and* to respect his relentless love extended to all. That's celebrating God's new way, *without* any Grade A Choice Religion.

PART 5

FRANK LLOYD WRONG

**We do not even know ourselves
except through Jesus Christ.**
Blaise Pascal (1623–1662)

15

W e're lost. I think we took a wrong turn off I-95. We're now in Norfolk instead of Richmond. But we should be there soon!" the hearse driver assured my mother on the phone. My mom hung up the phone, looked at her watch, and sighed, "I think we're in for a *long* wait."

We were standing at what was supposed to be my grandmother's graveside service. For the last forty minutes, the minister, my relatives, and I had been standing around the grave, just sort of staring at each other, wondering what to do. None of us had ever been to a funeral without the casket!

After another hour of waiting, the minister was growing restless. He said he had to be somewhere else soon. "If the hearse doesn't show up shortly, I'm not sure what we're going to do."

Rather than have a funeral without a casket *or* a minister, we decided to begin the service. The reverend made it all the way to the part where he was to commit my grandmother's body to the grave. "Ashes to ashes . . . ," he said, then stopped. "I can't really go any further without her body actually being here!" he said. "I'm sorry."

Just as he turned to leave, the hearse arrived. It screeched to a halt near the graveside, and out popped a bearded lady in a pin-striped, three-piece suit. It wasn't a full beard, but it was the beginnings of a respectable one by any standard, complete with mustache.

"So sorry I'm late! I took a wrong turn and went north instead of south. But I'm ready to do the ceremony," she said, brandishing a script she'd pulled from her coat pocket. "It's my first time, but I've got notes here."

"Do the ceremony?" my mother asked, her normally calm façade beginning to show a few cracks. "What are you talking about?"

The bearded lady looked puzzled. "That was part of the package—I transport the deceased, *and* I do the ceremony," she insisted. "You're going to have to pay for it anyway."

My mother paused and struggled visibly for control. Then she informed the driver that our family would pay the fee but that my grandmother's minister, who was standing right there, would be finishing the service.

The bearded lady hearse driver deflated a bit but delivered my grandmother's casket to us and drove away.

And the funeral, from that point on, really went off without a hitch.

Late to Your Own Funeral?

My grandmother had never been late a day of her life. But she was, as they say, late to her own funeral—literally.

In the same way, many of us are late to our funerals. I'm not speaking of the physical, of course, but of the spiritual. Both Romans and Galatians tell us that we *died* with Christ:

> For we know that *our old self was crucified with him* so that the body of sin might be done away with, that we should no longer be slaves to sin—because anyone who *has died* has been freed from sin. (Rom. 6:6–7)

> *I have been crucified with Christ and I no longer live*, but Christ lives in me. The life I live in the body, I live by faith in the Son of God, who loved me and gave himself for me. (Gal. 2:20)

Spiritually speaking, we participated in a funeral—our own. But we need to "attend" that funeral, to witness it and be aware of its implications.

In all our talk about behavior, spiritual disciplines, and self-improvement within Christianity, I'm afraid we neglect the core message of the Christian faith—death and new life. At its root, Christianity is really about dying and waking up a brand-new person. A fundamental exchange occurs within us at the moment we place our faith in Jesus Christ for salvation. Through our own death, burial, and resurrection, we become righteous saints, children of God. And this change is real and actual, not symbolic or figurative.

We participated in a funeral—our own.

There's a whole lot more to the new covenant than simply escaping law and being under grace. Grace won't work for just anybody. It's only intended for those who've been made new at the core. It's our newness in Christ working with the freedom of grace that unleashes expressions of God's Spirit.

WHY DIE?

"Why did we have to die with Christ? Isn't that a bit dramatic?" you might think. "Couldn't God have done it another way?"

The New Testament tells us that we died with Christ for good reasons. First, we died *to the law* so we could live in a new way (Gal. 2:19; Col. 2:20). Second, we died *to the power of sin* so we would have a free choice (Rom. 6:2, 7, 12). Third, we died to receive a *new heart*, a *new mind*, and a *new spirit*—to become a new creation (Ezek. 36:26; 1 Cor. 2:16; 2 Cor. 5:17). Some of us talk about how we "gave our life to Christ." In actuality, we had no life to give. God could not use our life. Instead, he crucified our old self and gave us a new life, his life.

The spiritual person we were in Adam was killed and laid in the tomb with Christ. "Well, yeah, *positionally*, but . . ." And there we go with our theological jargon. It's quite popular to hear that the death of our old self is only "positionally" true (true "in God's eyes" or true in heaven, but *not* a present reality here on earth). But there's no scriptural basis for seeing the death of our old self as only "positional truth."

I understand why we've done it: to explain our ongoing battle with sin. For similar reasons, some also say that we Christians need to "die to self." This implies that our

death with Christ is progressive, not yet complete. We'll
address the die-to-self theology in the next chapter, but
first, there's more.

THE OTHER HALF

God didn't leave us in the tomb. He went further in raising us up with Christ and seating us right next to himself
(Eph. 2:6). Did you catch where we are? Seated, right
next to God. Again, that's real—not symbolic or fake.
So how close are you to God? Because you've been joined
to Jesus (Rom. 6:5; 1 Cor. 6:17), you're right
next to God. You've got the best seat in the   **Apparently,**
house! Yes, it's a spiritual location. But   **we've already**
spiritual truth is very real truth. Everyone   **hit heaven.**
is somewhere spiritually—either in Adam
or in Christ. Your spiritual location is literal and actual.
It's from this spiritual reality that we are to live everyday
life on planet earth:

> And God raised us up with Christ and *seated us with him
> in the heavenly realms* in Christ Jesus. (Eph. 2:6)

> Since, then, *you have been raised with Christ*, set your
> hearts on things above, where Christ is seated at the right
> hand of God. Set your minds on things above, not on
> earthly things. *For you died, and your life is now hidden
> with Christ in God.* (Col. 3:1–3)

Did God mean for us to read about truths like these but
only experience them when we hit heaven? Apparently,
we've already hit heaven. Did you catch that? We're *already*

there spiritually, raised and seated with the King. So heaven is a place we're going, but heaven is a place we're already seated. Ever gone anywhere that you're already seated? Hmmm, we'll need to think on that one some more. But that's exactly what God would have us do—*think* on it:

> *Set your minds on things above*, not on earthly things. For you died, and your life is now hidden with Christ in God. (Col. 3:2–3)

BEING OURSELVES

Too often, we Christians presume that we're "sinners" at the core just like everyone else. In doing so, we ignore one of the greatest aspects of the cross—the killing off of our old self. When we take on the "I'm a dirty worm" theology and then seek to "be like Jesus," we'll find it to be a losing effort. Christianity then becomes an exercise in futility and falsehood. We're essentially trying to act like someone that we don't believe we are.

It then becomes religion.

We died. We've been raised and seated. And we're clean and close to God. What more can we ask for? But here's how we find ourselves praying: "Lord, I want to be closer to you." Yes, we're growing in our *knowledge* of God and his love, but here's an important truth: *we are already as close to God as we'll ever get.* Yes, that's right. If you're in Christ, then you're spiritually united with Jesus (Rom. 6:5) and seated right next to the Father (Eph. 2:6). But there's more—your human spirit is literally and actually fused with God's Spirit:

But the one who joins himself to the Lord is *one spirit* with Him. (1 Cor. 6:17 NASB)

One spirit with him? Now, that's close. Jesus made us new at the core, fusing his own Spirit to our new human spirit. We are to recognize this closeness, count on it as true (because it is true!), and live from it! This is different from the popular religion of *trying* to get close and stay close to God. And as we begin to grasp the beauty of our union in Christ, every motive we have will begin to change. We'll begin to see that living the Christian life is really just *being ourselves*.

16

In the film *Weekend at Bernie's*, Richard and Larry are best
friends trying to get ahead in their corporation. Along
the way, they discover that someone has been embezzling
money from the company. When they inform their company president, Bernie Lomax, he pretends to be pleased
with their discovery. So Bernie invites the young men to
his beach house as a way of thanking them.

When they arrive at the beach home, they discover Bernie
dead, apparently killed by the mafia. The young men soon
learn that Bernie himself was the embezzler and the mafia
was his partner in crime!

Then events take a turn toward the bizarre. Instead of
calling the cops, Richard and Larry concoct a scheme to
pretend Bernie is *still alive*. Dragging the corpse alongside
them wherever they go, they try to somehow continue with
the beach weekend of their dreams. But things get even
crazier when the mafia thinks Bernie is still alive and they
try to kill him all over again.

Although this makes for an entertaining film, it's a hor-
rible way to live the Christian life! As new creations, we're
not dragging around the corpse of our old self. Imagine
thousands of Christians limping along, dragging their
own personal Bernie at their side. That's a sad image!
But it's essentially what many of us have believed—that
we're dragging our old self along with us through life.
I guess we're thinking maybe someday, in heaven, we'll
finally be free.

Thank God the truth is better than that!

Black Dog on the Altar?

Realizing our death with Christ *as a finished work* is very
different from the idea of trying to "take up our cross"
and somehow "die to self." The die-to-self theology
would have us buy into the idea that we're dirty, sinful people who must rid ourselves of our selves, little
by little. That way, we can display Christ to the world.
Essentially, we must progressively be removed from the
equation.

This martyr-like religious philosophy ignores a simple
fact: at salvation, we have *already* been crucified (past
tense) with Christ (Gal. 2:20; Rom. 6:6; Col. 3:3). Not only
that, but the phrase "die to self" is *nowhere to be found
from Genesis to Revelation*. Despite its absence, it seems
to be choice theology for today's Christians to explain
their current fight with temptation. An analogy often given
involves a black dog and a white dog—two selves within
us. We need to feed the white dog (the new self) and starve

the black dog (the old self). Another popular way to put it is that we keep putting our old self on the altar to be sacrificed, but it keeps crawling off!

While these analogies are creative, they send the wrong message. They don't teach the truth of who we are as new creations in Christ. We weren't put on an altar. We were crucified on a cross. Interestingly, crucifixion is a type of death that you cannot bring upon yourself. God could have planned for Jesus to die by any means. I believe he chose this particular death for Jesus (and for our old self) so that we would see the futility of trying to crucify ourselves. Imagine trying to crucify yourself! You nail one hand up—then what? We didn't play a role in our crucifixion, and we cannot add to what God has already accomplished on our behalf. Whether it's Romans telling us "our old self was crucified" (Rom. 6:6) and that it was "once for all" (Rom. 6:10–11), or whether it's Galatians communicating that we were "crucified with Christ" (Gal. 2:20), or whether it's Colossians telling us that we "have taken off [our] old self" (Col. 3:9), the message is the same.

Imagine trying to crucify yourself! You nail one hand up—then what?

It is finished!

DEATH BY WILD BEASTS?

But doesn't Paul say "I die daily," and doesn't that mean we should too? Although the phrase "die daily" is often used to justify a die-to-self theology, *this passage has nothing to do with the old self or our struggle with sin*:

And as for us, why do we *endanger ourselves* every hour?
I *die every day*—I mean that, brothers—just as surely as
I glory over you in Christ Jesus our Lord. If I *fought wild
beasts* in Ephesus for merely human reasons, what have I
gained? (1 Cor. 15:30–32)

This is Paul defending his apostleship. He reminds his
readers that he and the other apostles endanger themselves every hour, even fighting wild beasts in Ephesus.
The apostles were doing whatever was needed to spread the
message. When it came to Paul's commitment, he literally
faced *physical* death daily.

Wow! The context for the phrase "die daily" sure sheds
light on the misconception many of us have had about
needing to die daily.

TAKING UP YOUR CROSS

But doesn't Jesus say that we should take up our cross and
follow him? And doesn't taking up our cross imply that
we need to die to self or at least die further to sin? It's true
that Jesus tells his audience to "take up your cross." And
that's part of the *salvation* message:

Then he called the crowd to him along with his disciples
and said: "If anyone would come after me, he must deny
himself and take up his cross and follow me. For whoever
wants to save his life will lose it, but whoever *loses his
life for me and for the gospel* will save it. What good is it
for a man to gain the whole world, yet *forfeit his soul?*"
(Mark 8:34–36)

The context of Jesus's statement about taking up our cross is so that we can *save our life and not forfeit our soul*. Clearly, Jesus's comments relate to salvation. So the question is: When do we get put on a cross? When are we crucified by following Jesus to his cross? The answer from Scripture is clear—at *salvation*. At salvation, we die with Christ (Rom. 6:6; Gal. 2:20), and this act needs no repeating.

There's no New Testament passage that implies we need to die to sin further (after salvation) or that we need to die to self at all. In fact, we actually see the opposite—our *once for all* death to sin is emphasized:

> The death he died, he died to sin *once for all*; but the life he lives, he lives to God. In the *same way*, count yourselves dead to sin but alive to God in Christ Jesus. (Rom. 6:10–11)

Our job is to recognize our one-time death to sin as being real. That way, it can have tangible effects in our thinking right here and now. If we fail to see this miraculous exchange as having already taken place, we'll live under the delusion that we're no different from a lost person. We'll end up thinking of ourselves as "sinners saved by grace" rather than grasping the radical truth that we're now saints *by nature*.

Spiritual Schizophrenia?

So if we're going to look for a reason why we still sin, we'd better not resurrect the old self in our theology. To do so goes against God's Word. And consider this: if you don't believe your old self is dead, buried, and gone, you're going to try to kill off "half of you" somehow. Jesus said that *a house divided against itself* cannot stand (Mark 3:25). Having two opposing identities at war with each other is a spiritual schizophrenia we can't stand. We're meant for something simpler. We're meant for something better. We're meant for *the truth*.

We are new.

We're now saints by nature.

There's one obstacle to us buying into this spiritual exchange of personhood as real and actual: the fact that *we still sin*. So some say our death with Christ is only positional ("heavenly") truth. Others say it's only progressive truth (becoming true, little by little). I guess we'll say whatever we need to say to explain why we still sin. After all, how can this heart surgery be anything more than progressive or symbolic if we still wake up every day and struggle?

Fortunately, there's an answer. It comes straight from the pen of the same apostle who informed us we're new. Paul tells us we're new, and then he tells us why we still struggle. And *why we still sin as new creations in Christ* is one of the most powerful discoveries any Christian can make. Over the next few chapters, we'll look to God's Word to make that discovery.

But first, let's talk politics.

17

In the United States, when a new president comes into office, he or she inevitably inherits problems created by the previous administration. It just comes with the territory. If the economy is spiraling into a depression, it could be due to the previous administration. If the unemployment rate is high, it might be because of the previous administration. If we're at war and things aren't going well, it may have something to do with the decisions made by the previous administration.

When most presidents come into office, they replace the previous cabinet with new staff. That way, old ways of doing things are eradicated, and the new president starts with a clean slate. The last thing a new president wants is old thinking in the White House.

No, it's time for change in Washington.

Although prior administrations have an impact on a new presidency, the American people don't like the blame game very much. The way we see it, a president is hired to fix our country's problems, not to throw the blame on the previous administration. They're gone. They're out of office. Some effects may be left over, but that's no excuse to dwell on the past.

Similarly, we have inherited the effects of our old self's presidency. Former choices have resulted in patterns of thinking and strategies for living stored in the cabinet of our minds. This is what the Bible calls *the flesh*. The flesh is the old way to think and the old way to act. In essence, the flesh is the policies of the previous administration.

> The flesh is the policies of the previous administration.

Now that the old self is out of office, dead and gone, we shouldn't pretend he's still around. We shouldn't engage in the presidential blame game by saying, "I couldn't help it. It was my old self!" No, we're in a new era, a time in which there's been an exchange of leadership. Sure, there are leftover effects, strategies, and ways of thinking—the flesh—but we are the new self:

> Therefore, if anyone is in Christ, he is a new creation; *the old has gone*, the new has come! (2 Cor. 5:17)

SINFUL NATURE?

In the New International Version (NIV), the term "sinful nature" is sometimes used to describe the source of our ongoing struggle. The trouble with that translation of the Greek word *sarx* is that it's easy for us Christians to assume that *our nature is sinful*. We equate "my sinful nature" with the idea that "my old self or my old nature is still around."

The literal translation of the word *sarx* is "flesh," not "sinful nature." Paul never intended us to think that the flesh is the old self come back to life. A study of the term "flesh" reveals that it's a way to *think* (Rom. 8:6) and a way to *walk* (Rom. 8:4 NASB)—it's the leftover programming we have from before salvation. This is why we need our minds renewed. We have fleshly *thinking* that needs reprogramming over time.

Before salvation, we had an intricate web of strategies for coping with life, dealing with pain, and getting what we wanted. But now we have a new way to think and a new source to draw from—the Spirit of God. If we fall back on the old way of thinking, it doesn't mean our old spirit has risen from the grave. No, it just means we're still getting our minds renewed.

Although our spirit (innermost being) houses our righteous nature in Christ, our soul (mind, will, emotions) doesn't contain any spiritual nature in itself. The soul (Greek: *psuche*) is just our psychology. The soul is like a mirror that reflects the flesh or God's Spirit in any given moment. It's our "soul mirror" that enables us to walk by the flesh or walk by the Spirit from one moment to the next.

So how do we "grow"? We learn more about who we *already* are as new creations in our spirit. Then we begin to allow our thoughts and actions to *reflect this spiritual reality* more each day. Only then are we really being ourselves!

So don't let the term "sinful nature" fool you. The publishers of the NIV note that "flesh" is the more literal translation. God's message about who we are as his children is consistent. We've died. We've been raised to newness of life. But we still struggle with old attitudes, old ways of coping, old programming. That's the flesh.

If we walk according to the flesh, it doesn't change the fact that our nature is new. It doesn't change our new source for life. It just means we're acting like someone we're not. We're choosing an old *way* when we as people are already made new.

FLAVORS OF FLESH

There are many flavors of fleshly thinking. As one example, the flesh may strategize to make us look good, sweet, and religious. Here we see Paul's flesh fabricating a religious résumé, based on his law keeping:

> If anyone else has a mind to put *confidence in the flesh*, I far more: circumcised the eighth day, of the nation of Israel, of the tribe of Benjamin, a Hebrew of Hebrews; as to the Law, a Pharisee; as to zeal, a persecutor of the church; as to the righteousness which is in the Law, found blameless. (Phil. 3:4–6 NASB)

That's one flavor of flesh—religious flesh. As we assemble an impressive résumé of religious performance (and subtly let people know about it!), we walk according to the flesh. This may include seeking to get value and identity from our denomination, our seminary education, our accomplishments at church, our "holy living," or our Bible smarts.

The flesh also pushes us toward self-improvement and goal setting so that we can see how far we've come and feel good about our "growth." Check out this passage as Paul reveals the self-improvement flavor of flesh:

> Are you so foolish? Having begun by the Spirit, are you now being *perfected by the flesh*? (Gal. 3:3 NASB)

Perfectionist flesh seeks to grow us and improve us. Like the religious flavor of flesh, perfectionist flesh wants to make us look good, not bad.

Although religious or perfectionist flesh may look and feel right, God isn't asking us to fix or improve ourselves. Instead, we're to continue just as we started in Jesus, growing with "a growth which is from God" (Col. 2:19 NASB). This is different from the strategies employed by self-improvement flesh. One way leads to pride, stress, and burnout. The other way leads to life and peace (Rom. 8:6). If we find ourselves burned out on church activities and good behavior, we haven't understood the difference between religious or perfectionist flesh and walking in the freedom of God's Spirit (2 Cor. 3:17).

Perfectionist flesh seeks to grow us and improve us.

Not all of us struggle with self-improvement flavors of flesh. There are other manifestations of fleshly thinking that seek temporal pleasure at a shallow level. The flesh gravitates toward self-focused thoughts, attention-getting strategies, and carnal desires. Here's a snapshot of some ugly flavors of flesh: immorality, jealousy, outbursts of anger, envying, and disputes or divisions (Gal. 5:19–21).

No matter what the flavor of flesh, its desires are against what God is doing in our life. *The flesh hinders us from seeing who we really are in Christ* and from doing what we truly please:

> For the flesh sets its desire against the Spirit, and the Spirit against the flesh; for these are in opposition to one another, *so that you may not do the things that you please.* (Gal. 5:17 NASB)

THE THIRD WAY

So how do we stop the flesh? Thank God we're not to spend our days examining the flesh, trying to rid ourselves of it. No, the flesh and its way of thinking won't disappear until heaven. So rather than having an obsession with inspecting the flesh, we're to have one *simple* focus:

> But I say, walk by the Spirit, and you will not carry out the desire of the flesh. (Gal. 5:16 NASB)

Does this mean we "let go and let God" and "we get out of the way" so that "it's all of him and none of us"? This might sound right at first. But do you hear what I hear? Those who say this think they're *incompatible* with God's purposes. They must rid themselves of themselves so God can act in their lives. All of God and none of us? What about the truth that we've been re-created? As new creations, we've been *united* with Jesus Christ. Are we really supposed to get out of God's way?

God wants to embrace us, not replace us.

No, we're supposed to be in the midst of it all. God wants to embrace us, not replace us. After all, if we're in Christ, he *already* replaced us at salvation! We are new, righteous, holy saints, entirely compatible with God's Spirit. He embraces our personalities, our senses of humor, even our hobbies and interests. He expresses *his* life through these unique aspects of our personhood.

Because of the timeless heart surgery of the cross, God is now shouting from the rooftops, "You are one hundred percent acceptable to me!" When we hold on tightly to the idea that God is right about our new identity, we walk according to truth. When we set our minds on the truth about ourselves and our true desires, we *automatically* avoid walking by the flesh.

Religion prods the flesh to either try harder with perfectionist flesh or give up and resort to immorality. It's only when we see our union with Jesus Christ that we understand there is *a third way* to live. It's not by trying harder, and it's not by giving in to immorality. It's a life motivated by the freedom of grace that releases God's Spirit to be all we need in every moment.

18

About six months after we moved into our new home in South Bend, Indiana, the phone bill arrived as it usually did. This month, though, we were in for a surprise.

"Nearly a thousand dollars? In calls to a psychic hotline? My wife has lost her mind." That was my first guess when I saw the phone bill. It turned out Katharine had seen the phone bill too and was equally concerned about me!

Our first reaction was laughter, which soon turned into concern. How would we prove we didn't make the calls? We certainly couldn't afford to pay the bill!

We called the phone company, and they sent someone to investigate. When the telephone man arrived, we explained that we'd received a bill for calls we didn't make. He asked to see the bill. After looking at it for a few seconds, he said, "You know, you can call the psychic hotline, and they'll let you enter the day and time of the calls on your bill. Then you can hear their recording of the actual call."

We grabbed the phone, dialed the hotline, and typed in the day and time of one call on our bill. "Chantal Abbott," the lady on the recording said after the psychic asked for her name. And that's all the hotline would let us hear—just the first fifteen seconds of the call. Then we punched in a few other days and times, and for each call we got the same name.

"It was some lady named Chantal Abbott," I announced. The telephone man seemed intrigued and scurried off to do some checking around our house. A few minutes later, he came back. He hadn't found anything but said he was headed down the street to where all the phone lines on our block come together.

"I'll let you know what I find. This is fun!"

"Fun?" I wondered, "Maybe fun *for him*." For us, the whole thing was bizarre and even a bit scary. By this time, we weren't exactly settling in comfortably to South Bend culture.

The telephone man returned twenty minutes later with a gleam in his eyes and said, "I checked at the corner where all the lines come in. Sure enough, there's something going on. There are notch marks in the telephone pole where someone has been climbing up pretty regularly. And when I climbed up, I saw that the insulation had been cut away from the bundle of phone lines, and it's *your* line that is exposed. Apparently, someone's been tapping into your line and making calls."

"There's more!" he said excitedly. "I noticed that one house near the pole didn't have phone service, so I suspected they might be the ones tapping your line. Then I asked somebody walking by on the street if they knew who lived in that house. They didn't know her last name but said her first name is Chantal."

All of the calls were made late at night. Apparently, a lady named Chantal was climbing a telephone pole in the middle of the night. She was using some kind of spiked shoes to climb up, and then she was clamping into our phone line to call a psychic. Well, what better way is there to test the authenticity of a psychic? Just ask them, "Where am I right now?" as you're suspended twenty feet in the air on a telephone pole!

The telephone man said he'd make sure the calls were removed from our bill. He also said we could report Chantal to the police, but we decided not to. As long as the charges were taken off the bill, we didn't really care.

But the phone company must have cared. Within forty-eight hours, a moving truck had pulled up in front of that corner house and Chantal was nowhere to be found!

Perhaps she moved on the advice of the psychic?

WHO'S TAPPING YOUR LINE?

I tell you this true story to demonstrate how easy it is for someone to infiltrate our lives and take over our lines of communication without us even realizing it. And the same thing can happen to us spiritually.

It's easy for our *minds* to get tapped.

The result is "calls" that are not ours, even though they may sound just like us. The calls may tempt us to do things we know are wrong. The calls may run scenarios through our minds, offering suggestions on how to get payback for what someone did to us. Or the calls may flood us with fear as we entertain all the "what ifs" of life.

There's a power called *sin* (*hamartia* in Greek) that actually dials in and does the talking. Sin is cold and calculated in its attempt to sway us. It's a crafty agent that clamps on to our lines, placing all kinds of calls. These calls fill us with religious pride, or make us worry about our future, or get us down on ourselves. Once we realize these calls are being placed, we need to examine them through the filter of God's truth about us. Does this thought fit with *my true identity* as a new creation? Is it consistent with *a loving God* who counsels and comforts me and has forgotten my sins?

If not, then the thought is from a *third* party.

If we accept those calls as our own and go ahead and pay the bill, we're buying a lie about the type of people we are. We're children of the living God. We're not of this world. We are a people of God's own possession. When we give in to the calls of sin, we've failed to realize that someone is tapping our line.

THE "OTHER" SIN

Most of us think of the word *sin* as a verb, an action. But *Vine's Expository Dictionary of Old and New Testament Words* reveals a second use of the word *sin* that has a meaning all its own. According to W. E. Vine, sin is a governing power that operates through the members of our body. Vine also asserts that this governing power carries person-like characteristics. Here sin is a noun, not a verb.

God is telling us that *there's a personified power called sin that acts through our bodies.*

In short, someone is tapping our line.

The first we see of this personified power is when God warns Cain, "*Sin* is crouching at your door; *it* desires to have you, but you must rule over *it*" (Gen. 4:7 TNIV). Then, in Romans 6 and 7, we see this word *sin* (Greek: *hamartia*) popping up all over the place. Paul tells us that sin is housed within our bodies, right under our noses (not literally), and causes us to do what *we* don't really want to do:

> Therefore do not let *sin* reign *in your mortal body* so that you obey *its* lusts. (Rom. 6:12 NASB)

> So now, *no longer am I* the one doing it, but *sin* which dwells in me. (Rom. 7:17 NASB)

> But if I am doing the very thing I do not want, *I am no longer the one* doing it, but *sin* which dwells in me. (Rom. 7:20 NASB)

Did you notice to whom the lusts belong in that first verse? Romans 6:12 says, "*its* lusts." Paul is claiming that something in us, that is *not* us, is the source of temptation. And the lusts we so often struggle with belong to *it*!

Note that the power of sin resides in our physical body. At salvation, nothing happens to our *bodies*. Therefore, sin's ability to tap into our minds remains the same.

The Romans 7 experience of "doing what I don't really want to do" will be ours any time we give law-based religion

Someone is tapping our line.

our best shot. *God introduced the law so that we might discover the presence of this rogue agent within.* If we choose law religion, it will inevitably dawn on us, "No matter how hard I try, I find that I'm addicted to sin."

The power of sin thrives under the law. But, in God's wisdom, he caused us to die to the law, and we therefore *simultaneously die to sin.* The heart surgery we received at salvation cuts our ties with sin and allows us the freedom to finally choose something else.

But if we don't understand what happened to us at salvation, we may mistake the messages of sin for our old self. Instead of calling ourselves critical spirits, we need to recognize the critical thoughts as coming from sin. Instead of calling ourselves dirty or perverted, we need to know that lustful thoughts have an organized power called *sin* as their source. Instead of calling ourselves (or others) gossips, we can realize that it's this sin principle within that would have us act in such a way.

Recognizing the source of temptation is a big deal.

Recognizing the source of temptation is a big deal. It enables us to see how we can be new creations at the core but still struggle with sin. It also helps us understand why a rule-based religion always results in failure as it only excites this power called sin. We're meant to be motivated by grace from deep within our human spirit.

We're meant for God *without* religion.

19

One winter we went away on vacation and came home to a very cold house. Both the upstairs and the downstairs furnaces appeared to be broken, so we called a professional. Within a few hours, the repairman was at our front door. After a few minutes of inspecting our heating systems, the technician came in the house with a look of disbelief.

"You've got to see this!" he said.

We followed him out to the furnaces in our garage, where he pulled the front panels off to reveal shredded plastic all over the interior. A rat had found his way inside both heating units, and he had eaten through all the condensation tubing. Once pressure was lost in the tubes, the furnaces automatically shut down.

After parts and labor, that rat cost us nearly $1,000 in damages. Then we put out poison and set traps. But it was only two weeks later that the varmint teed us up for another $2,500 in damages. This time he ate his way through an upstairs bathtub pipe that flooded our first-story ceiling!

To this day we're not certain if the rat will return to wreak more havoc or if we managed to get him. But if we ever do find the rat, we plan to stuff him and mount him!

After all, that's a $3,500 rat.

THE RAT IN YOUR HOUSE

I share this story with you because there's a rat in your home too. The power of sin is a rogue agent that's living in your house, your human body. And just like our rat did, sin can wreak lots of havoc. As new creations we're dead to sin. But sin itself is still very much alive, just like that rat was still alive after we thought we'd killed it.

Imagine if the repairman had never discovered the damage or we had never attributed it to the rat. Maybe my wife and I would've blamed each other, perhaps even buying the idea that one of us had programmed the thermostat wrongly, or forgotten to change the filter, or even gone out to the furnace and chopped up all the tubing. That may sound silly, but similarly we Christians can beat ourselves up over the actions of the rat: "I'm a sincere Christian. I want to know God better and grow spiritually. So why do I keep dealing with these same old thoughts over and over again?" It's crucial to recognize that there's something *in* us that's *not* us. There's a force housed within our physical body that both tempts us and then controls us if we allow it. The source of our sins is a rat called *sin*.

Did you know there's a rat in *your* house?

THE SOURCE OF SINFUL THOUGHTS

Many of us assume that we are the sum total of our thoughts, that *we are what we think*. But God is tipping Satan's hand by revealing that there's the presence of another. Not every thought we think comes from us. Not every idea that our minds are served originates with us.

I used to think that the loudest and most persistent thoughts in my head were from me. Of course they are, because I'm thinking them! Therefore, when temptations continued to nag, it must be me. My *nature* is showing itself to be sinful. I must be dirty at the core.

> Did you know there's a rat in *your* house?

But by discovering the spiritual rat in my house, I can now see that I should judge a thought not by its volume or frequency but instead by its *content*. No matter how persistent a thought is, I can recognize that it is simply that rat once again trying to cost me a fortune in damages.

Our God is calling us to reinterpret every ounce of our thought life in light of what he has revealed. I'm a new creation, a child of God, with a new heart, a new mind, a new spirit, and God's Spirit living in me. When we realize our newness, trust in it, and act on it, we live in reality. And the reality of our newness is confirmed, again and again, since thinking "God thoughts" is the only choice that fulfills us. Why? Because we have *the mind of Christ* (1 Cor. 2:16)!

FRANK LLOYD WRONG

My wife Katharine and I were married right after graduate school. We weren't working with a large budget for our first home, but we knew we wanted something unique. After driving our real estate agent crazy for several weeks, we were ecstatic when she finally stumbled on a for-sale-by-owner 1908 Prairie-style home. It was designed by a student of Frank Lloyd Wright, the famous American architect. Surrounded by traditional Victorian painted ladies, this house stood out from the rest. In fact, it was registered with the local historical society and on the city's historical tour. The city respected the unique design of this home so much that it had been moved from its original spot and preserved when a hospital needed the land.

Frank Lloyd Wright–style homes of that period are characterized by unique features such as low-pitched rooflines, overhanging eaves, and rows of casement windows. Our home was no exception. It was a genuine period piece and a privilege to own.

Imagine, though, that once we move in, I start getting some ideas about how to improve the place: "We could take out those windows and put in a sliding glass door. We could rip out those horizontal lines and add some gingerbread décor along the eaves so it looks more like other houses on the street. And we could frame up a new roofline so it's not so flat anymore."

Then I grab a sledgehammer and go to work.

Of course, that never happened. I would have made a mockery of that house. We owned a unique piece of architectural history that would've been ruined if I had tried to "improve" it. You don't purchase a historical home designed to reflect a certain style and then try to force it into a different genre. That's turning Frank Lloyd Wright into Frank Lloyd Wrong.

As children of God, we are perfectly designed by the Master Architect. But we're so convinced of our own unworthiness, so obsessed with our failures, that it's hard for us to believe we don't need to be "fixed." Blinded by the flesh's desire to self-improve, we may not see how out of place our attempts to perfect ourselves really are. Sure, there's "yard work"— changes in our *attitudes* and *actions*—as we "put on love" each day (Col. 3:14). But there's an important truth to be understood here: we—who we are structurally at the core—cannot be improved. We are the Master's handiwork, created in Christ Jesus as a new species of heavenly people:

> **We are perfectly designed by the Master Architect.**

> For we are *God's workmanship*, created in Christ Jesus to do good works, which God prepared in advance for us to do. (Eph. 2:10)

> But you are a *chosen* people, a *royal* priesthood, a *holy* nation, a people *belonging to God*, that you may declare the praises of him who called you out of darkness into his wonderful light. (1 Pet. 2:9)

The whole purpose of the gospel is to communicate that we are in need of Jesus for genuine change. This fundamental change happens when we receive Christ. It's our job from that day forward to learn about the masterpiece that God has fashioned us to be. We are told *to live from our perfection in Christ* rather than trying to "perfect ourselves" through religion:

> In the same way, *count yourselves dead to sin* but alive to God in Christ Jesus. (Rom. 6:11)

> Are you so foolish? Having begun by the Spirit, *are you now being perfected by the flesh*? (Gal. 3:3 NASB)

> For by one offering He has *perfected for all time* those who are sanctified. (Heb. 10:14 NASB)

God has crafted us into a beautiful home for himself. Once we realize this, it's only natural for us to accept ourselves just as he does. If we see ourselves as an old, dilapidated shack, we'll be driven to constantly make structural changes. And these self-inflicted "improvements" run counter to God's intent for us. We can't improve upon the work of a Master Architect. We are the product of God's finest workmanship.

And you don't mess with a masterpiece.

20

In my "God without Religion" seminar, I ask people a series of questions to see what they think of themselves. I ask them to measure themselves against people we know or have heard of.

I first ask, "How many of you would say you're as righteous as me?"

Most hands go up. Some people even wave two!

I then raise the bar. "How many are as righteous as Mother Teresa?"

A lot of hands go down, but a few confident ones remain. "God probably grades on a curve, and I just don't have her opportunities, but if I did . . ." they might think.

I up the ante even more. "How many are as righteous as the apostle Paul?"

Only a few brave souls persist.

Then I deliver the final blow. "And how many are as righteous as Jesus Christ?"

With that one, I'm lucky to see one hand remaining.

But here's the deal: if we can't say, "I am as righteous as Jesus Christ," then we've missed it. We've missed the whole point. Maybe we've admitted our righteousness is a gift, but we've never really *owned* it.

When it comes to righteousness, many of us rightly believe in imputed righteousness—that God is counting us as righteous. But we might mistakenly think that righteousness is not real and tangible, at least not here and now.

Maybe we've admitted our righteousness is a gift, but we've never really *owned* it.

Maybe we imagine that God is up in heaven pretending that we're righteous. Perhaps he sees us out of the corner of his eye as he looks upon Jesus instead. If he were to turn in our direction and really look at us, he'd see that same old dirty sinner that we still are.

Yes, we're *clothed* with Christ's righteousness. But don't you dare look under those clothes or you'll be in for a ghastly surprise! Or maybe God will give us a last-minute polish just before we reach the pearly gates. But wait—there's only talk of us getting new *bodies* in heaven, so when do we ever become 100 percent clean and right on the inside, in our human spirit?

Could it be *now*?

IMPUTED OR IMPARTED?

There's a sense in which imputed righteousness is certainly true. We've been declared righteous through Christ. And we've had righteousness credited to our account (Gal. 3:6–7). But there's so much more to it! We've had righteousness not only imputed to us but also *imparted* to us. Everyone agrees that our old self was literally and actually *un*righteous by nature. Likewise, after the death of our old self, we were raised to be a new self—who is *literally* and *actually* righteous by nature. That's the news flash!

Jesus said it well. He stated that our righteousness had to compete and win against the Pharisees in order to enter heaven (Matt. 5:20). So if we are heaven-bound people, then how righteous are we? Imagine thousands of Pharisees all lined up with their lifelong efforts lying beside them in a heap. All the blood, sweat, and tears that Pharisees experienced to try to get right with God pales in comparison to the righteousness we possess freely in Jesus Christ. The righteousness we possess is greater than all of the Pharisees' efforts combined.

Why doesn't the Bible speak of a last-minute polish for Christians just before we hit heaven? Because right here, right now, we are as righteous as we'll ever be. Sure, we'll get new bodies some day. As far as our human *spirit* goes, though, we're ready for heaven. And our *soul* (psychology) is like a mirror that can reflect anything—sin or righteousness—in a given moment. It too is ready for heaven where there will be no sin to reflect. Together, our spirit and soul are already equipped for heaven, right now. It's just our bodies that'll need replacing.

So we're as righteous as Jesus Christ in our human spirit. That's what is so radical about the gospel:

God made him who had no sin to be sin for us, so that *in him we might become the righteousness of God.* (2 Cor. 5:21)

"Well, yeah, *in Christ*," we might say as we shove the idea to the wayside. We end up agreeing that we're righteous *in Christ*, as if that's not quite real. So is God pretending our new birth is a reality? Is God pretending we have a new heart? Is God pretending we're righteous? Or does he call us "the righteousness of God" because it's actually true?

Righteousness won't do us any good unless we own it. And when we relegate it to some bin of truth that's not quite real, it becomes useless to us in the everyday. It's true that we received Christ's righteousness as a gift. But what should you do with the greatest gift you've ever been given?

Own it.

HEART-TO-HEART TALK

Do you have a sinful heart? I can't tell you how many Christians I've met who would answer yes to that question. Then they remark, "But I'm saved by grace." Now, that may sound really humble to you, but do you see what I see? There's a fundamental problem with believing that Christians have a sinful heart. The whole point of being reborn in Christ is that we get a new heart (Ezek. 36:26), a new mind (1 Cor. 2:16), a **Do you have a** new spirit (Ezek. 36:26; Rom. 8:16), and **sinful heart?** God's Spirit living in us (1 Cor. 3:16). We might think it's a humble, spiritual thing to say that our hearts are wicked, but God does not want us to be deluded. He longs for us to recognize the effects of our resurrection in his Son—an inner transformation that changed our hearts forever.

"The Bible calls us sinners!" some will say.

Well, not really. If you're a Christian, the New Testament repeatedly calls you a saint, not a sinner.

"But Paul said he was the chief of sinners!" some reply.

It's true that Paul wrote to Timothy, "Christ Jesus came into the world to save sinners—of whom I am the worst" (1 Tim. 1:15). However, context reveals that Paul was referring to his track record in killing Christians, *before* salvation, when he was "a blasphemer and a persecutor and a violent man" (1 Tim. 1:13). Here Paul is remarking how gracious God was in forgiving him and calling him to serve as an apostle. Paul was reborn as a saint, after having been a chief of sinners *in his past.*

Although Paul's meaning is fairly straightforward, it's funny how we Christians will grasp at nearly any verse we can find to justify continuing in a poor self-image. We seem to be infatuated with wallowing in guilt while perceiving ourselves to be dirty sinners saved by grace. We end up believing that we *should* live uprightly, but we really don't want to deep down. But, because of our rebirth, I dare you to consider the following thought:

I never really want to sin.

Of course, we Christians can and do sin. That's not what I'm talking about. What I'm saying is that we don't *want* to sin. If we're in Christ Jesus, we're re-created for good works (Eph. 2:10), and sin is just awkward and unproductive for us (Rom. 6:21). If we want to make ourselves uncomfortable, there's one surefire way to do that—by sinning. Sinning goes against everything in our being:

No one who is born of God will continue to sin, because God's seed remains in him; he cannot go on sinning, because he has been born of God. (1 John 3:9)

Now, I know what you've heard: sin is the stuff we want to do but aren't supposed to do. What I'm saying is, that's wrong. Sin is totally *incompatible* with who we are, and it's the last thing we want to do:

For the flesh sets its desire against the Spirit, and the Spirit against the flesh; for these are in opposition to one another, *so that you may not do the things that you please.* (Gal. 5:17 NASB)

Did you notice the two "teams" in this passage? There's the flesh on one team, and then there's you and the Spirit of God on the other team. The flesh's goal is to keep you from doing "the things that *you* please."

Apparently, we want what God wants. He has imprinted his desires on our hearts: "though you were slaves of sin, you became *obedient from the heart*" (Rom. 6:17 NASB). For the rest of our lives, we'll continue to prove our new birth, one way or another. We'll prove it by expressing Christ and being fulfilled, or by sinning and being miserable.

Either way, we prove our true identity.

WAKING UP CANADIAN

Through a series of laws enacted decades ago, many Canadian-born children lost their citizenship when their parents decided the family should move to the United States. It's estimated that more than one hundred thousand Canadians were affected.

Recently everything changed. Thanks to years of petitioning by just a small number of people, one morning in 2005, thousands of people literally woke up Canadian. The Canadian government restored citizenship to those who had previously lost it. Thousands of letters went out announcing to those affected, "As of today, you are officially a Canadian citizen."

Our human spirit became compatible with God's Spirit.

In the same way, we lost our spiritual citizenship in the Garden of Eden. When our ancestor Adam abandoned God's kingdom, the human race was transferred to a land of separation and darkness. Through receiving Christ Jesus, we're restored to citizenship in God's kingdom. But lots of us still aren't really aware of our newfound citizenship and its implications. Maybe we never got the letter, or maybe we received it but didn't quite understand what it all meant.

God says there's been a spiritual transfer from our being *in* Adam to being *in* Christ:

> But *by His doing* you are *in* Christ Jesus, who became to us wisdom from God, and righteousness and sanctification, and redemption. (1 Cor. 1:30 NASB)

> For He *rescued us* from the domain of darkness, and *transferred us* to the kingdom of His beloved Son. (Col. 1:13 NASB)

With this miraculous transfer came a radical change at the core of our being. Our human spirit became compatible with God's Spirit. He now literally resides there, just beneath our humanity. We're literally and actually born of God, equipped with everything we need for a new life. And we actually participate in God's divine nature!

> His divine power has given us *everything we need for life and godliness* through our knowledge of him who called us by his own glory and goodness. Through these he has given us his very great and precious promises, so that through them *you may participate in the divine nature* and escape the corruption in the world caused by evil desires. (2 Peter 1:3–4)

In 2005, one hundred thousand people woke up Canadian. It's time we Christians wake up and realize who we are. We've got a new spiritual lineage and a new citizenship. And it's our newness in Jesus Christ that liberates us from any need for religion.

21

Daddy, what does it mean to be baptized?" Lindsey said.

My friend Steven had an opportunity he didn't want to waste. His young daughter Lindsey was asking him about baptism and what it all means.

"Let's go over to the kitchen sink," Steven said. "And bring that water bottle."

Steven plugged one side of the sink and filled it with water. Once the water was deep enough, he shut it off. He took the empty bottle and held it over the sink.

"What's going to happen when I drop this bottle in the water, Lindsey?"

"It'll fill up with water," she replied.

"And will it float or sink?" Steven asked.

"It'll sink all the way to the bottom," she said.

"That's right, Lindsey. And this is a picture of what happens to us when we believe in Jesus," Steven said as he let the bottle fill with water and sink to the bottom. "We're baptized spiritually into Christ. He is in us just like the water fills this bottle. And we're in him, just like the bottle is in this water. The water is in the bottle, and the bottle is in the water. But there's one more thing we need to do."

Steven reached across the counter and grabbed the bottle cap. He put his hands down into the water and screwed the cap on the bottle, leaving it submerged with water inside.

> **Baptism is a beautiful picture of our death, burial, and resurrection in Christ.**

"After God fills us with the Spirit of Jesus, he seals us until his return. He'll never leave us. We're in him and he's in us, permanently."

That day, Lindsey got one of the best lessons anyone can get on the true meaning of water baptism, right there at the kitchen sink.

COLOR ME PURPLE

Baptism is a beautiful picture of our death, burial, and resurrection in Christ. Our *spiritual* baptism is portrayed and celebrated with water baptism:

> Or don't you know that all of us who were *baptized into Christ Jesus* were baptized *into his death*? We were therefore *buried with him* through baptism into death in order that, just *as Christ was raised* from the dead through the glory of the Father, *we too* may live a new life. (Rom. 6:3–4)

As we're lowered into the water, this depicts our death with Christ. And as we're lifted out of the water, this symbolizes our being raised to newness of life. But I believe there's even more to appreciate about water baptism.

Perhaps its deepest meaning can be understood better by examining an ancient tradition that took place long before any Christians were ever baptized.

Thousands of years ago, ancient dye workers would crush sea snail shells to form a purple powder. Once the powder was mixed with water, it became a very effective purple dye. Then the workers would dip their fabric into a large jar of this purple dye. Naturally, the fabric would take on the purple color of the dye as it was "baptized" into the dye.

The color purple has traditionally been associated with royalty in both Greek and Roman societies. When a white cloth is immersed in purple dye, the cloth itself takes on a new status, a new identity. A common cloth emerges from the dye transformed and with a new purpose.

Christians use this same word, *baptism* (from the Greek *baptízō*, meaning "dip" or "immerse"), to describe our tradition of being immersed in water. The term implies that we go down into the water and we emerge as a person publicly *identified* with Christ. Baptism is also a picture of us becoming royalty, as we are a royal priesthood in Jesus Christ (1 Pet. 2:9). Before, we were a fabric for common use. Through being placed into Christ, we became new creations, transformed with a whole new purpose.

We are set apart for the King.

Holy Water?

"We know you've been baptized, but you need to be baptized in *our* water," the pastor said. "Baptism is about identifying yourself with the one true church. Getting baptized in our water will assure you of that. There's no genuine salvation without it."

Kathleen was confused. She had put her faith in Jesus Christ for salvation as a teenager, and she had been baptized shortly after. Now a pastor was telling her she needed to do it all over again, *in his church*. On top of that, he was saying there's no real salvation without water baptism.

Could that be right?

Baptism is just one of the many issues that has divided the church. One denomination says to sprinkle. Another says to dunk. One says it's necessary for salvation. And another, as Kathleen witnessed, even claims you must be baptized in *their* water for it to really "count."

Throughout history, religious people have sought to separate themselves through *external* acts. In the first and second millennia, many have attempted to set themselves apart for God by changing their names, cutting their hair, wearing special robes, or even removing themselves from society. Today, some Christians try to set themselves apart for God (and from so-called weaker Christians) by associating with an exclusive denomination, by idolizing a particular teacher, or by immersing themselves in the latest trendy movement. Others see themselves as "super Christians" based on how much they read their Bibles, share their faith, serve at church, or impact the world.

We as humans naturally gravitate toward *external, visible* means of determining where we are with God. Our divisions and disputes over water baptism are a sign that we don't realize we're *already* set apart *in* Christ, not through anything outward.

Baptism as Religion

As far back as the Corinthian church, we see believers dividing over baptism. Back then, it wasn't disputes about the method of baptism. It was all about the perceived "greatness" of the baptizer himself. "I was baptized by Peter himself! Who baptized you?" they'd say. Paul confronted these Corinthian status seekers, saying:

> Is Christ divided? Was Paul crucified for you? Were you baptized into the name of Paul? *I am thankful that I did not baptize any of you* except Crispus and Gaius, so no one can say that you were baptized into my name. . . . For *Christ did not send me to baptize*, but to preach the gospel—not with words of human wisdom, lest the cross of Christ be emptied of its power. (1 Cor. 1:13–15, 17)

If water baptism brought salvation, Paul would've been *very* busy baptizing! Instead, we find him saying the opposite. He spent very little time baptizing, because God didn't send him to baptize. Apparently, it was hearing and believing the gospel that brought salvation, not baptism.

We see this in Paul's reasoning with the Galatians: "Did you *receive the Spirit* by observing the law, or *by believing what you heard*?" (Gal. 3:2). It's clear from this passage and others (see Acts 10:47) that the apostles taught that we receive the Spirit by believing, not by water baptism.

> If water baptism brought salvation, Paul would've been very busy baptizing!

We know that baptism is biblical. The apostles baptized new believers throughout the book of Acts. But what's the

173

proper place of baptism in our lives? And how can we keep it from becoming divisive religion?

MEET MACK, MEET MAKER

Imagine a person who trusts in Christ for salvation after hearing the gospel at church one Sunday morning. On his drive to lunch, he's tragically killed as a Mack truck meets his car head-on. He meets his Maker. At the gate of heaven, he's turned away. Although he expressed faith in Christ's death and resurrection to save him, he failed to get baptized in water. Therefore, he burns in hell forever.

Sound absurd? Large groups of Christians around the world adhere to a religion that teaches exactly that. It may be a misunderstanding of this statement by Jesus that got it all started:

> Very truly I tell you, no one can enter the kingdom of God *without being born of water and the Spirit.* Flesh gives birth to flesh, but the Spirit gives birth to spirit. (John 3:5–6 TNIV)

Some interpret this passage to mean there's no salvation without baptism in water. But is this really what Jesus meant?

Jesus is talking about two births, one natural and one spiritual. Anyone who's ever had a baby knows the first sign that labor has begun in earnest is when the sac of water encasing the baby breaks. This is why Jesus describes our natural birth as being "born of water." He then contrasts it with a second, spiritual birth that is being "born of the

Spirit." To drive this point home, he then says, "flesh gives birth to flesh, but the Spirit gives birth to spirit" (John 3:6).

All humans are born of water. For most of us, this requirement is met shortly after our mother reaches the hospital. To meet Jesus's second requirement, all that's needed is a spiritual birth. Water comes into play at our first (physical) birth. At the second birth, it's the Spirit himself, nothing physical, that brings our newness.

God is about what happens on the inside. As Peter shows us, getting wet for sixty seconds is not what saves us:

> Baptism *into the resurrection of Jesus Christ changes us forever.*

> *Baptism now saves you—not the removal of dirt from the flesh*, but an appeal to God for a good conscience— *through the resurrection* of Jesus Christ, who is at the right hand of God, having gone into heaven, after angels and authorities and powers had been subjected to Him. (1 Pet. 3:21–22 NASB).

Notice that two types of baptism are being contrasted here. There is a baptism that saves, but it is not the kind with water that removes dirt from your body. It is another type of baptism. Baptism *into the resurrection* of Jesus Christ changes us forever.

Now that's something to celebrate publicly and for eternity!

PART 6

GOVERNMENT BAILOUT

Forgiveness of sins is the very heart
of Christianity, and yet it is a mighty
dangerous thing to preach.

Martin Luther (1483–1546)

22

In 2008, the global economy suffered a massive blow. The US mortgage crisis was threatening millions of households and the stock market. The government eventually stepped in and approved a national mortgage bailout plan. This plan allowed some homeowners to be relieved of the responsibility of their mortgage loan.

But rest assured, the banks got paid. Whether it was paid to them by the homeowner or by the government, the banks received their money. That's just the way the world operates.

Prior to the government bailout, I'm sure that thousands of homeowners found themselves down at the bank apologizing and begging for mercy. They may have shed tears, pleaded their case, and even made offers to pay the bank another way.

But one thing is for sure: the banks didn't care. Why not? Because any debts incurred in our country's financial sector are paid back with one type of currency: money. Not apologies. Not explanations.

Money.

We've got a *money*-based economy.

GOD'S BLOOD-BASED ECONOMY

When it comes to forgiveness, God has always endorsed a blood-based economy. Under the old covenant, it was blood that brought atonement, yearly. Under the new, it is blood that brought us our forgiveness, once for all:

> The law requires that nearly everything be cleansed with blood, and *without the shedding of blood there is no forgiveness.* (Heb. 9:22)

God's blood currency appears in both the old and the new. The difference between the two comes down to one question: *How many times was blood shed?* Under the old, blood was shed over and over. Under the new, Jesus's blood was shed only once:

> Unlike the other high priests, [Christ] does not need to offer sacrifices day after day, first for his own sins, and then for the sins of the people. He sacrificed for their sins *once for all* when he offered himself. (Heb. 7:27)

Big deal! So what? We all know that Jesus only died *once.*

True. But not all Christians are on the same page about just how forgiven we are. If blood is the only way to be forgiven, and Jesus won't shed his blood ever again, then we need to ask: How forgiven am I? And do I need to do anything to get any more forgiven?

On planet earth, we don't normally work with a blood economy. The way it usually works is that I forgive you when you show up on my doorstep with tears in your eyes and an apology on your lips. I forgive you when you recognize your wrongdoing. I forgive you when you promise to do better. But that's not God's way. It never has been. Under the old or the new, it has never been an apology-based system. It's always been about blood.

> Do I need to do anything to get any more forgiven?

"If I'm a parent, I want my children to come to me and ask me for forgiveness. Then I'll tell them I forgive them," some might say. We assume there's a parallel between our ways and God's ways. I certainly understand the temptation to draw upon familiar analogies. And I agree that an apology-based system is what we see in human relationships such as parenting. But do you see the difference? Our human interactions don't involve our perfect Son suffering and dying a bloody death to take away our sins once for all.

In short, *we aren't God*. And our ways are *not* his ways.

The Takeaway

Imagine a Jewish man traveling home after the Day of Atonement. He's just participated in the temple sacrifices. What relief! What gratefulness to God! Another 365 days of sins are covered.

The man gets home only to find his wife nagging him for being gone so long. In his frustration and anger, he lets one slip. He uses the Lord's name in vain. Now it's 365 more days before that sin will be taken care of. And he's just getting started. An entire year of sinning will take place before he feels relief again. For thousands of years, this Jewish system of forgiveness was in force:

> Moses said to Aaron, "*Come to the altar and sacrifice your sin offering* and your burnt offering and make atonement for yourself and the people; sacrifice the offering that is for the people and *make atonement* for them, *as the* LORD *has commanded.*" (Lev. 9:7)

Just as Moses instructed, the same sacrifices were offered, year after year, that could never really cleanse anyone:

> The law is only a shadow of the good things that are com- ing—not the realities themselves. For this reason *it can never, by the same sacrifices repeated endlessly year after year, make perfect* those who draw near to worship. If it could, would they not have stopped being offered? For the worshipers would have been cleansed once for all, and would no longer have felt guilty for their sins. But those sacrifices are an annual reminder of sins, because *it is im- possible for the blood of bulls and goats to take away sins.* (Heb. 10:1–4)

Those sacrifices never took away sins; they only atoned for a year's worth. And they were really just an annual reminder of sins (v. 3), since covering sins (atonement) is not enough. Sins must be *taken away* to be truly forgiven.

That's what made John the Baptist's words so special as he shouted, "Look, the Lamb of God, who *takes away the sin of the world!*" (John 1:29). The new, perfect Lamb had come on the scene to take away sins, not merely cover them. "Atonement" is *not* a new covenant concept. The word in Greek for what Jesus accomplished is *hilasterion,* meaning "the gift that propitiates or satisfies completely." The term "atonement" doesn't appear even once in the New Testament to refer to what Jesus accomplished on Calvary. Jesus did more than atone for our sins. He gave us a gift in his death that took away our sins, satisfying God forever!

Religion says get right with God—daily, weekly, yearly.

Of course, this meant the sacrificial system could stop. Any Jewish person who believed in Jesus could fold up shop in the temple. Why? "For the worshipers would have been *cleansed once for all* and would *no longer have felt guilty* for their sins" (Heb. 10:2). There's no more need for guilt when the sin issue is over. But again, how can we be certain that the sin issue is over? Because Jesus's blood sacrifice needed no repeating:

> Christ was sacrificed *once* to *take away* the sins of many people. (Heb. 9:28)

Religion says get right with God—daily, weekly, yearly. Whether it's the tribal religion where they're marching around the fire once a season; or the Jewish religion where they're marching their way to the temple once a year; or a Catholic religion where they march their way to the weekly Mass; or a Protestant religion in which they march down the aisle, again and again, to ask for forgiveness and "get right"—it's all the same. They're marching, over and over, to get right and *stay* right.

And that's religion.

But God adheres to a *blood*-based economy. Because Jesus Christ shed his blood only *once*, we Christians are forgiven people. This means we can refuse to join in the religious parade. We can step out of that marching line. We can stand firm, knowing that "it is finished" (John 19:30).

God says Jesus is the one and only satisfying sacrifice (1 John 2:2). God is completely satisfied with the sacrifice of his Son. If God himself is satisfied, who are we to argue with him?

No Second Thoughts

Because God is satisfied, Jesus won't come swooping down out of heaven to die again. Nor is Jesus up in heaven being crucified over and over:

> *Nor did he enter heaven to offer himself again and again,* the way the high priest enters the Most Holy Place every year with blood that is not his own. Then Christ would have had to suffer *many times* since the creation of the world. *But now he has appeared once for all* at the end of the ages to do away with sin by the sacrifice of himself. (Heb. 9:25–26)

If God isn't planning any repeat sacrifices on earth or in heaven, it can only mean one thing: our past, present, and future sins have been completely obliterated! We are not *being* forgiven progressively and in danger of God having some second thoughts. No, we've *already* been forgiven, past tense:

> Be kind and compassionate to one another, forgiving each other, just as in Christ God *forgave* you. (Eph. 4:32)

> God made you alive with Christ. He *forgave* us all our sins, having canceled the written code, with its regulations, that was against us and that stood opposed to us; he took it away, nailing it to the cross. (Col. 2:13–14)

> And where these *have been forgiven*, there is no longer any sacrifice for sin. (Heb. 10:18)

Passages like these, written in past tense, show that our forgiveness is an accomplished fact. It's not something ongoing or in progress. It's done.

Just stop and think about it for a minute. How many of your sins were in the future when Christ died? All of them! The sins you committed prior to salvation, the sins you committed after salvation, and the sins you'll commit tomorrow were *all in the future when Jesus died* and took them away. God made no distinction with regard to time of occurrence. This means we *have been* forgiven—past tense—of *all* our sins.

How many of your sins were in the future when Christ died?

We are forgiven people.

23

I'd like you to think of two numbers. The first is the number of sins you've committed in your life. Okay, just make a rough guess. Got it? Now, the second number is the number of those sins that you've *confessed* or *asked forgiveness for*.

See the problem? One of those numbers is a lot smaller than the other. It seems we can only remember and confess a fraction of the sins we've committed. But the Bible tells us that God is a holy God who can't tolerate sin. So how could we enter heaven with any sins—forgotten or remembered—that haven't been entirely dealt with? For this very reason, *our forgiveness is not contingent upon any act of our own* (our confession, our repentance, or our asking for forgiveness).

No, our forgiveness is *solely* based on the blood of Christ.

Confession or asking for forgiveness cannot possibly be a condition for becoming forgiven. We've already forgotten about thousands of sins in our lives. God's redeeming work through the cross isn't contingent upon our memory, the listing of our failures, or even our expressions of sorrow over what we've done.

THE AMNESIA SOLUTION?

"But isn't confession needed under 'normal' circumstances *in order to be forgiven*? Sure, God doesn't concern himself with sins we've forgotten. But what about the ones we still remember doing?"

This may sound plausible on the surface. But there's no biblical reason for distinguishing confessed sins from unconfessed sins. And there's no difference between remembered sins and forgotten sins. If sins we've forgotten were no longer on God's radar simply because we've forgotten them, the best solution would be for us to contract some sort of spiritual amnesia. If we forget them, apparently the God of the universe forgets them too!

Is that what the Bible actually teaches? Not at all. Our forgiveness is not dependent on our memory, our words, our confession, or our asking. Our forgiveness rests solely on the "once for all" blood sacrifice of Christ. And there's no mention of any last-minute cleansing that we get right before we hit heaven.

But what if my life is taken before I can confess, repent from, or ask for forgiveness for a sin? Catholic priests offer confession and communion at your deathbed. Since they teach transubstantiation, they hold that bread and wine literally become the body and blood of Christ. So communion translates into a last-minute, *blood*-based forgiveness before you meet your God.

Miss out on that, and you may be out of luck.

Although this concept ignores the "once for all" nature of Christ's sacrifice, at least it's more consistent than some of our muddy Protestant thought. It shows some understanding of God's economy, that

All three systems ignore what the Bible clearly teaches.

only *blood* brings forgiveness. However, the big Catholic mistake is equating wine with blood. Doing so communicates that Christ's blood and the corresponding forgiveness are doled out in portions, over and over. This is hardly different from the Old Testament atonement (covering of sins) provided through animal blood once a year.

So the Catholic obtains more forgiveness and cleansing weekly through the Mass. The Jew obtained more forgiveness and cleansing yearly at the Day of Atonement. And many Protestants believe in a *word*-based economy, thinking they receive more forgiveness and cleansing as they *ask* God directly for it. But all three systems ignore what the Bible clearly teaches—God's blood economy that brought "once for all" forgiveness and cleansing through the one-time sacrifice of Jesus (Heb. 7:27; 9:26). Any of our systems—whether Jewish or Catholic or Protestant—that ignore God's blood economy and the "once for all" sacrifice of Jesus Christ are innately flawed.

The truth is simple. We've been forgiven—past tense (Col. 2:13). And we've been cleansed—past tense (Heb. 10:2). Here's how the God of the universe puts it:

Then he adds: "Their sins and lawless acts *I will remember no more*." And where these *have been forgiven*, there is no longer any sacrifice for sins. (Heb. 10:17–18)

THE LORD'S PRAYER

But what about the Lord's Prayer? Jesus says, "Forgive us our sins *as we have forgiven* those who sin against us." Everyone's jaws dropped when they heard that one. Jesus was saying here's how to pray: "God, please give me the same amount and type of forgiveness that I've passed on to others." Then in the conclusion to Jesus's prayer, he really hits them hard. He warns that they won't be forgiven *unless* they go around forgiving others first:

> For *if you forgive others* for their transgressions, your heavenly Father will also forgive you. But *if you do not forgive others*, then your Father *will not forgive* your transgressions. (Matt. 6:14–15 NASB)

That's right. Jesus tells his Jewish listeners that their forgiveness is *conditional* upon their forgiving others first. Take a moment. Read the Lord's Prayer slowly, especially the ending and the conclusion. Now compare it, for example, with these passages written *after* the cross:

> Be kind and compassionate to one another, *forgiving each other*, just as in Christ God *forgave* you. (Eph. 4:32)

> Bear with each other and *forgive whatever grievances* you may have against one another. Forgive as the Lord *forgave* you. (Col. 3:13)

Jesus said "forgive us our sins as we have forgiven those who sin against us" *before* the cross. He modeled the Lord's Prayer *before* his blood was shed. And it's a prayer that will condemn anyone. If we were to receive forgiveness from God that only mirrored our own forgiveness of others, we'd be doomed. On this side of the cross, our forgiveness isn't gained by forgiving others first. Forgiveness is a gift in Christ, with no strings attached. We pass forgiveness on to others because we *already* have it in Christ.

Jesus's prayer was designed to expose our hopelessness apart from grace.

No Asking Needed

Jesus's prayer was designed to expose our hopelessness apart from grace. God wants us to realize that we're going to need more than just the same kind of forgiveness we've been passing out to others. God wants us to see his forgiveness *as a gift*, not something earned through forgiving others first.

God's forgiveness isn't about listing every sin on a legal pad, asking for forgiveness, and then getting cleansed. Yes, it's very religious to ask for forgiveness and rely on our own ability to confess everything. But it denigrates the work of the cross. Jesus took away our sins and cleansed us "once for all." To ask, plead, beg, and wait for cleansing that we've already been given is to ignore what Jesus said from the cross: "It is finished" (John 19:30).

24

There's still one big worm in the apple when it comes to understanding our unconditional forgiveness and cleansing:

> If *we confess our sins*, he is faithful and just and will forgive us our sins and purify us from all unrighteousness. (1 John 1:9)

No other verse has caused more damage to Christians' assurance of their forgiveness. If we take that opening phrase out of context, our whole understanding of God's unconditional forgiveness can fall to pieces. It's all too easy to interpret this verse to mean that God responds, daily, to our confessions by doling out new portions of forgiveness and cleansing. God forgives us Christians *only if we confess our sins*, we might think.

But this is *not* the context of 1 John 1:9.

Let's examine this verse a little closer. First, this verse *is* a conditional statement. The passage includes a conditional "if" marker and additional grammar (in subjunctive mood) that indicates an uncertainty about whether someone will decide to confess. And there's a corresponding uncertainty about whether they'll be forgiven and cleansed. They'll be forgiven if they confess, but *they will not be forgiven if they don't confess.*

Now, ask yourself: Is this true for a Christian? If it is, then we must throw every other passage on forgiveness out the window. And we need to begin first-John-one-nining weekly, daily, even hourly so that we don't accidentally miss a sin.

So what's the deal with 1 John 1:9?

GNOSTIC HERESIES

When we crack open our Bibles, we often assume that the verses we read must be addressing Christians. We forget that the early church was composed of believers, unbelievers, those on the verge of believing, and outright heretics. At that time, there weren't a dozen denominations to choose from in a given city. There was one church, and it contained everyone remotely interested in the gospel, along with all their right and wrong beliefs.

Any apostle knew this. So in writing to the early church, they would often say things directed at unbelievers with the hope that they'd come to faith in Jesus. John's first chapter is certainly one of these cases. Notice what John's hope is for them:

> We proclaim to you what we have seen and heard, *so that you also may have fellowship with us.* And *our* fellowship is with the Father and with his Son, Jesus Christ. (1 John 1:3)

The audience John is addressing *does not have fellowship* with the Father and the Son yet. John is proclaiming these things to them *so that they can have fellowship also*. Why don't they have it yet? What's preventing them? As we read further, we find out:

> If we *claim to have fellowship* with him yet walk in the darkness, we lie and do not live by the truth. . . . If we *claim to be without sin*, we deceive ourselves and the truth is *not* in us. . . . If we *claim we have not sinned*, we make him out to be a liar and his word has no place in our lives. (1 John 1:6, 8, 10)

In this passage, John is addressing early Gnostic heretics who claimed to be sinless. Gnostics were also pushing the heresy that Jesus didn't come in the flesh. They claimed that God would never take on a lower form, even for a short time. God is only spirit, they said, and he would never appear in real human flesh. Therefore, they believed Jesus to be an illusion of sorts. Maybe you could put your hand right through him like a beam of light.

John is addressing early Gnostic heretics.

In John's epistle, he addresses this early church heresy. He says anyone who denies the physicality of Jesus is "not from God" (1 John 4:3). In addition, he opens his first chapter by saying:

> That which was from the beginning, which we have *heard*, which we have *seen* with our eyes, which we have *looked at* and our hands have *touched*—this we proclaim concerning the Word of life. The life appeared; we have *seen* it and testify to it, and we proclaim to you the eternal life, which was with the Father and has appeared to us. (1 John 1:1–2)

Notice how many times John uses physical words to say that he witnessed Jesus's physicality. John opens his letter by driving home the fact that Jesus did come in the flesh. Who would this message be for? Remember that anyone who denied Jesus's physicality was "not from God" (1 John 4:3). John is obviously addressing *unbelievers* at the beginning of his letter.

Interestingly, Gnostic heretics *also* claimed that sin wasn't real or didn't matter. Therefore, they claimed to be sinless. These Gnostics are precisely who John addresses in his first chapter. And John says they don't have the truth or God's Word in them:

> If we claim to be without sin, we deceive ourselves and *the truth is not in us*. . . . If we claim we have not sinned, we make him out to be a liar and *his word has no place in our lives*. (1 John 1:8, 10)

Can we be sure that John is describing *unbelievers*? Yes. In another letter, this same author (John) tells us that we Christians *do* have the truth in us and that the truth will be with us forever:

> The elder, to the chosen lady and her children, whom I love in the truth—and not I only, but also all who know the truth—because of *the truth, which lives in us and will be with us forever*. (2 John 1:1–2)

We Christians have the truth living in us, and the truth will be with us forever. Now compare that to the group back in 1 John who:

1. say they have no sin;
2. say they've not sinned;
3. do not have the truth in them; and
4. do not have the Word in them.

Imagine that I introduce you to a friend of mine: "I want you to meet my friend Dave. What's interesting about Dave is that he walks in darkness. Dave doesn't live by the truth. Dave claims to be without sin. Dave doesn't have the truth in him. Dave has made God into a liar, and the Word has no place in Dave's life. Other than that, Dave's a great guy!" After hearing my introduction and shaking Dave's hand, do you walk away concluding that Dave is a Christian? Of course not! The first step to becoming a Christian is *admitting you're a sinner*.

Is 1 John 1:9 addressing Christians? Absolutely not!

So is 1 John 1:9 addressing Christians? Absolutely not! In his opening chapter, the apostle John is addressing un-saved people like Dave who were living in denial about their sin. They didn't have fellowship with God yet. They couldn't experience total forgiveness yet. And they didn't know "once for all" cleansing yet. John's hope was that they would come to their senses. If they'd just admit their sin, then they could enjoy total forgiveness in Christ.

"My Little Children"

John transitions in his second chapter to address "My little children" (1 John 2:1 NASB). He then clearly tells Christians that "your sins *have been forgiven* on account of [Jesus's] name" (1 John 2:12). Christians are forgiven people, so John expresses our forgiveness in past tense, as a completed action.

So who needs to confess their sins *in order to be forgiven and cleansed* of all unrighteousness? The same people who've been running around claiming to be "without sin" (1 John 1:8). The same people who've been saying that they "have not sinned" (1 John 1:10). John is clearly addressing Gnostic heretics and anyone who has been following them—*un*believers.

First John 1:9 was never intended to be the Christian's "bar of soap" for daily cleansing. Instead, it was written as an invitation to the Gnostic heretic (or any other deluded soul) who might claim sinless perfection. Instead of believing that nonsense, John is asking them to admit and confess their sins to God. If they do, they'll enjoy forgiveness and cleansing of *"all* unrighteousness" (v. 9).

Notice John's use of the word *all*. Total, unconditional forgiveness and cleansing of *all unrighteousness* is what we receive in Jesus Christ. This verse was never meant to invite a one-by-one tallying of our sins. We don't get more and more forgiveness, progressively, throughout our lives. That would be Judaism all over again, dressed up in 1 John 1:9 clothes!

There's no system for getting more forgiveness or more cleansing.

Real forgiveness is simpler than that. Real forgiveness is "once for all" (Heb. 7:27; 10:10). We've been perfectly cleansed forever:

> For by one offering He has *perfected for all time* those who are sanctified. (Heb. 10:14 NASB)

"All Systems, No!"

First John 1:9 is a one of a kind verse. There's no other passage in any epistle that could even remotely be interpreted to mean that God's forgiveness of Christians is conditional upon our daily confession. If this were really our daily "bar of soap" system, wouldn't we find it clearly taught *to Christians* in various epistles? After all, remaining forgiven and cleansed before God is pretty important, don't you think?

The reality is that any system—whether Jewish or Catholic or Protestant or other—that requires us to *do something repeatedly* to maintain our cleansing will fail. We have forgotten about thousands of our sins, and they would go unforgiven and uncleansed.

Any system that does not take into account our "once for all" cleansing by the one-time sacrifice of Jesus Christ is an insult to God's finished work. We have either been forgiven (past tense) or we still need to be forgiven. They can't both be true. Once we put 1 John 1:9 in context as an invitation to the unbelieving heretic, all other forgiveness passages throughout the New Testament shout from the rooftops that we *have been* forgiven completely, unconditionally, and forever.

There's no system for getting more forgiveness. There's no system for getting more cleansing. There's no system for "staying right" with God. There's no system for "staying in fellowship" with God.

There is no system.

25

It was the first time we'd experienced communion with PowerPoint. The lights dimmed as the first slide appeared on the screen: "CONFESSION," it read in big block letters.

"Before we take of the Lord's Supper together, we need to get right with God. So we'll be guided through some confessions to make sure we're in right standing first. Then we'll partake together," the pastor said.

The service began with "Confession as a Nation." This was an opportunity for the congregation to repent and apologize to God for the ways America has strayed from its Christian roots. This was followed by "Confession as a Church," an opportunity for members of the church to confess our shortcomings as a congregation. After a couple of minutes, we participated in "Confession as a Family" and were asked to think of ways our family had fallen short in being salt and light and reaching people for Christ.

From there the pastor transitioned to "Confession as an Individual." We were then guided through a number of subcategories such as sins against a spouse, immediate family, relatives, co-workers, employers or employees, friends, and any other fellow church members. This was followed by a slide titled "Reconciliation" and an invitation to confess any sins against anyone attending the service itself.

"There are sins of commission and then there are sins of omission," the pastor continued. "We need to think about unconfessed sins that we've committed, but we also need to think about things we could have done but failed to do. These are sins of omission. Allow God to bring all of these to mind as well."

Although it was dark in the room, there was enough light to see that the mood around us was quite somber. It felt like a funeral. Some were bent over crying, while others were literally wailing. Many were milling around searching for folks they had wronged. Others remained hunched in their chairs with their faces buried in their hands.

After about forty-five minutes of guided confession, we were told that the pastoral staff would be up front. We could now come forward to receive the elements of the Lord's Supper if we felt "ready." However, it was made clear that if any unconfessed sins remained, we should *not* come forward at all but "let the cup pass us by."

It was a new church for us, and we left that service very discouraged by what we'd witnessed.

EXAMINATION INFESTATION

I'm all for confessing our sins to one another, but that isn't the purpose of the Lord's Supper. Jesus told us that we're supposed to celebrate the Lord's Supper in memory of *him*! To be specific, Jesus said, "Do this in remembrance of me" (Luke 22:19; 1 Cor. 11:24), not in remembrance of our recent track record. We're called to recognize the beauty of the "once for all" sacrifice of Jesus Christ that took away our sins and made us right with God. The focus is supposed to be on the Lamb of God and what he's done for us. Instead, we had attended an orgy of introspection, self-examination, and self-flagellation (without the scourges).

There's an explanation for today's popular religion of "getting right with God" before the Lord's Supper. It involves a misinterpretation of Paul's instruction to the Corinthian church. It's not uncommon for this passage to be used to justify the "dim the lights and introspect" approach:

> Therefore, whoever eats the bread or drinks the cup of the Lord in *an unworthy manner* will be guilty of sinning against the body and blood of the Lord. A man ought to *examine* himself before he eats of the bread and drinks of the cup. For anyone who eats and drinks without recognizing the body of the Lord eats and drinks *judgment* on himself. (1 Cor. 11:27–29)

These are some serious consequences. Sinning against the body and blood of the Lord, and bringing judgment upon yourself—of course we don't want to do that! So it sounds like we'd better examine ourselves before taking communion, right?

Wait. Before we jump to any conclusions, let's find out what Paul is really talking about. As always, context is our friend.

CORINTHIAN COMMUNION

Earlier in Paul's letter, we see him chastising the Corinthians for their lack of unity. Apparently, they're forming all kinds of cliques:

> I hear that when you come together as a church, there are *divisions among you*, and to some extent I believe it. (1 Cor. 11:18)

And these divisions are affecting the way the Lord's Supper is celebrated:

> When you come together, it is not the Lord's Supper you eat, for as you eat, each of you goes ahead *without waiting for anybody else*. One remains *hungry*, another gets *drunk*. Don't you have homes to eat and drink in? Or do you despise the church of God and *humiliate those who have nothing*? (1 Cor. 11:20–22)

Some were getting drunk. Others were showing up early and eating all the food. This can't happen in churches today. Why not? For starters, most of us ingest the equivalent of one shot glass of wine (or juice!) at a communion service. Secondly, we eat a single cracker, wafer, or piece of bread. It's just not possible to get drunk or be accused of gluttony when that's all you get.

This can't happen in churches today.

Two thousand years ago, things were different. The church in Corinth would gather regularly in someone's home for a multicourse meal and the Lord's Supper. They'd drink wine—real wine—and apparently some would even get drunk. Others would show up early and gorge themselves on the food, not leaving any for those who needed a warm meal the most—the poor. For them, a church gathering was a way to get nourished spiritually *and* physically.

Lately, though, the physical nourishment hadn't been possible. The poor would show up, and there'd be nothing left. Paul says, "one remains hungry, another gets drunk" (v. 21).

THE UNWORTHY MANNER

So what's the "unworthy manner" in which they were eating and drinking? It's pretty clear when you picture it. They weren't reflecting on the death, burial, and resurrection of Jesus Christ. They weren't using the bread and wine to remember him. Instead, they were consumed with being first, filling their own stomachs, and looking to alcohol as the cure for their emotional ails. Their eating involved gluttony, and their drinking involved drunkenness. They brought disgrace on the celebration itself. And a number of them were literally getting sick or maybe even dying of alcoholism:

> That is why many among you are *weak* and *sick*, and a number of you have *fallen asleep*. (1 Cor. 11:30)

Gluttony and drunkenness were the unworthy manner. This is why Paul gave the Corinthians this simple solution as he concluded his thoughts:

> So then, my brothers, when you come together to eat, *wait for each other*. If anyone is hungry, he should eat at home, so that when you meet together it may not result in *judgment*. (1 Cor. 11:33–34)

That's the whole solution: "wait for each other" and "eat at home." But what about the "judgment" mentioned here? Christians won't be judged or punished by God (John 3:18; 1 John 4:17–18). So what could this judgment mean? From the context, it's obvious that they were *judging each other*. This judging of each other was the source of their divisions and factions discussed in the previous verses:

> In the first place, I hear that when you come together as a church, there are *divisions among you*, and to some extent I believe it. (1 Cor. 11:18)

Imagine you're a poor member of the early church. You bring your family to a church meal, only to find that everyone else beat you to it. They're sprawled all over the place, complaining about how full they are. Some are even drunk or passed out. What would your reaction be? I'd be tempted to criticize, ridicule, and slander those who were "stealing" the food intended for my family: "Look at Aegeus! He doesn't care about us poor people. All he cares about is himself and his own family. Every time we gather, they're always the first ones here, and they end up eating platefuls of food, leaving none for us. And how about Xenos over there? He drinks even more than he eats! And he ends up passing out in his chair before we're done, drunk as a skunk."

This is why their church meetings together would "result in judgment" (1 Cor. 11:34). This is why Paul tells those who have plenty, "Wait politely for each other, and eat at home if you're really *that* hungry." That's how the passage concludes, because that's the whole solution to their problem.

What did they need to "examine"? The way they were eating and drinking at the Lord's Supper. What was the "unworthy manner"? Their gluttony and drunkenness! This passage isn't about some sort of required inspection of our sins in order to qualify for the Lord's Supper. In context, it was about the Corinthians needing to celebrate the Lord's Supper in the right way and for the right reasons. We're called to celebrate "in remembrance of [Jesus]," not in remembrance of our recent performance. To teach that we must first go through a purging or cleansing in order to partake of the bread and wine is *not* the meaning of this passage. And it is a disgrace to the finished work of Christ that has qualified us, once for all.

COMMUNION WITHOUT RELIGION

I began this chapter by telling you about our experience in visiting a church where religion took center stage during communion. I'd like to end by telling you a little about what the celebration of the Lord's Supper can be. If we're not supposed to spend all this time confessing, what do we actually *do*?

At Ecclesia, we combine the Lord's Supper with a message that centers on the finished work of Christ. We make it very clear *why* we are celebrating. The lights stay on. And there's no crying at all, at least no tears of sadness. We raise our glasses like you might see at a wedding toast. We pray. But our prayers aren't prayers of confession. They are prayers of thankfulness to God for what he did for us through Jesus. We do some examination, but it's the Lord's work on Calvary that we inspect.

We conduct the entire celebration in remembrance of Jesus. But with all of today's distortions of the celebration, we find it necessary to remind each other that it's *not about us*. It's not about our track record or some

> We should walk away feeling great, not guilty.

cleansing ritual. Instead, it's about what Jesus did for us. It should be more like a party than a funeral. And we should walk away feeling great, not guilty.

THE WHOLE POINT

The point of the Lord's Supper is to remind us how clean and how close to our God we really are. The work was entirely Jesus Christ's. He did a fantastic job of obliterating any record of our sins. God remembers our sins no more. So the Lord's Supper celebration is the *last* place we should be remembering them.

Are we really allowed to make it all about him and not about us? Yes! It's the only way to truly celebrate.

It's communion *without* religion.

26

So to sum this up—am I saying there's *nothing* for us Christians to do to get more forgiven, to get more cleansed, to get right for communion, or to remain in right standing with God?

Yes, I am.

But hang on a second before you slam this book shut.

Even though we don't confess our sins or ask for forgiveness *in order to be forgiven and cleansed*, we'll still find ourselves sorrowful after sinning. There's a godly sorrow (2 Cor. 7:10) we experience, because we've been re-created by God for good works. Our sorrow is not *just* regret that we didn't allow the Spirit to express himself through us (Eph. 4:30; 1 Thess. 5:19). It's also *from our own human spirit* that cries out to be an expression of Christ on this side of heaven (Rom. 8:23). We'll never be satisfied with sinning. We're made for something greater.

We're designed to express God's life.

"Tell Me What to Do!"

So what are we to do when we sin? We agree with God about our wrong choice. We thank God that this sin is one among the billions that were already taken away by Jesus's blood. We turn 180 degrees away from our sin (Rom. 6:12). We depend on God's Spirit for genuine change. If our sinful activity has left damage behind, we repair the damage if possible (Rom. 12:18). *But we don't have to ask or wait or hope for forgiveness to come our way, since this is equivalent to asking Christ to die all over again.*

Here's a practical example from Scripture. Some believers in the church in Ephesus were stealing, and the apostle Paul's advice was this:

> He who has been stealing must *steal no longer*, but must *work*, doing something useful *with his own hands*, that he may have something *to share with those in need*. (Eph. 4:28)

Seems like pretty practical advice, doesn't it? Did you notice how future-focused Paul was? He wasn't trying to get them to dim the lights and obsess over each and every theft. He wasn't looking for them to submit to some guilt trip over the whole thing. The apostle was essentially saying, "Spare yourself the fear and consequences from committing crimes. Get a job, have some respect for who you are, and do what's fitting for saints—share with those in need."

Paul's advice would be the same for us today. Rather than drumming up our past, he'd point us toward a future that is more fulfilling and more hopeful. He'd remind us that our destiny is expressing Jesus Christ in everything.

So here's the bottom line. Yes, we should agree with God that our sinful behavior is senseless. Yes, we turn from every sin we commit. And yes, we are to be honest and open with God and with others who will pray for us (James 5:16). But we should also move forward in confidence concerning what the blood of Jesus accomplished. We possess an unconditional, irrevocable, one-time cleansing from all our sins!

SECRET IN THE SLAMMER

Rick had committed murder and gotten away with it. He sat in his prison cell day after day, holding the secret inside.

He'd been locked up for years for a lesser crime but would soon be released. Although the police suspected Rick had committed the murder, they didn't have enough evidence to pin it on him.

> We should agree with God that our sinful behavior is senseless.

While in prison, Rick came to know Christ.

Then the idea of confessing his crime began to well up within him. Still, he couldn't bring himself to jeopardize his upcoming release by admitting to the murder. That'd give the police what they needed to lock him up for life.

So he kept his secret inside.

One day, two men entered the prison with a message of total, unconditional forgiveness in Jesus Christ. Rick had already received Christ, but as he soaked up the grace-filled teaching from these two men, he realized just how forgiven and free he really was.

my side," he said, "and if God is for me, then
what does it matter if anyone else is against me?" With a
deeper understanding of his forgiveness and acceptance in
Christ came a desire for truthfulness in every area of his life.
And the most natural result was to confess to the murder
he had committed years ago.

Rick's sentence was extended. He still sits in prison today
because of that confession. But Rick knows he did what
the Spirit of God and his own spirit within him desired. He
feels the relief of being honest and open about his crime.

ANTI-CONFESSION?

The two men who entered that prison are friends of mine.
They know the gospel and teach it in a clear and simple
manner. It was their presentation that freed
Rick to confess his crime.

The message of total, unconditional forgiveness is sometimes misunderstood as anti-
confessional. Nothing could be further from
the truth. Although it's not our confession,
our sorrow, or even our repentance that cleanses us before
God, confession is healthy and natural for the Christian.
Confession of our sins is simply agreeing with God and
choosing the truth over a lie.

There's a place for confession, both to God and to others. James tells us to confess our sins to one another and
pray for one another so that we may be healed (James
5:16). Some people pay a hundred dollars an hour to tell
someone their problems and find healing. The work of the

There's a place for confession, both to God and to others.

cross should mean we can share struggles with our spiritual Father and with like-minded brothers and sisters in Christ, at no charge.

Total forgiveness makes us clean and close to our God. Our cleanness and closeness gives us the confidence to be real with God and others. This also means that we can rightfully *choose grace* as we listen to the struggles of others and pray for them. This type of radical forgiveness shows us that God is in our corner, no matter what. With God himself on our side, we can have the courage to face the damage we've done, no matter what it might cost us in *this* world.

Rick found that out in his own life. Although he remains locked up to this day, he's now freer than ever.

PART **7**

THEATER OF LIFE

God's grace turns out men and
women with a strong family likeness
to Jesus Christ, not milksops.

Oswald Chambers (1874–1917)

27

Many of us enjoy air travel to our favorite destinations on a regular basis. But we probably don't think much about what goes into this luxurious convenience. It was on December 17, 1903, that Wilbur and Orville Wright flew the very first powered airplane over the sandy beaches of Kitty Hawk, North Carolina.

Even though the first flight lasted only about twelve seconds and covered a mere 120 feet, the Wright brothers were absolutely convinced that airplane flight was possible. They had made over seven hundred successful flights with gliders, and they had calculated how certain forces imposed upon a wing of a particular shape would allow a plane to lift off the surface of the earth.

Weren't the Wright brothers aware of the law of gravity? Of course! But they were counting on *other* principles to "overcome" that law.

Much like the law of gravity, there's a spiritual law of sin and death. Sin deserves death, every single time. But if we're in Christ, we are fortunate to enjoy life under a different principle. This greater principle *overcomes* the law of sin and death. It's called the law of the Spirit of life:

> Therefore, there is now no condemnation for those who are in Christ Jesus, because through Christ Jesus *the law of the Spirit of life* set me free from *the law of sin and death*. (Rom. 8:1–2)

Being under the law of the Spirit of life means we're not bound by the law of sin and death. When we sin, we don't experience the deserved punishment from God. Sure, we experience earthly consequences because of our poor choices. But this is different from receiving the one great consequence from the hand of almighty God.

Death fell on Jesus instead.

"IN AND OUT" THEOLOGY

Grace is a big buzzword these days, but we can't bring ourselves to believe in *this* kind of grace. It can't be true that we live in a permanently cleansed state with no strings attached! But here it is in black and white:

> By *one* offering [Jesus] has *perfected for all time* those who are sanctified. (Heb. 10:14 NASB)

We find ourselves believing in some lesser punishment for sin. We think that when we sin, God gets angry with us. Perhaps we envision him in a swivel chair as he rotates his face away, just until we get our act together. Some refer to this as being "out of fellowship."

The term "fellowship" appears a dozen times in the Bible. It describes our spiritual connection with God and other Christians. However, we often hear this term used as everyday religious jargon to describe our *feelings* of closeness to God at a given moment. We say we're "in fellowship" (right with God) or "out of fellowship" (not right with God) based on our recent performance.

Fellowship is *not* talked about this way in the Bible. There's not a single verse that talks about Christians going in and out of fellowship based on our recent performance. Instead, the term "fellowship" refers to regenerated saints who have fellowship with the Father, Son, and Holy Spirit (1 Cor. 1:9; 2 Cor. 13:14; Phil. 2:1) and with each other (1 John 1:3, 7). Those who do not have fellowship are lost. They walk in darkness, even if they *think* they have fellowship (1 John 1:6).

> We live in a permanently cleansed state with no strings attached!

We Christians are always in fellowship with God. Jesus was out of fellowship with the Father when he became sin on the cross. He did this so that we'd *never* be out of fellowship (Matt. 27:46; 2 Cor. 5:21; Heb. 13:5)! Our connection with God is certain and stable because of the "once for all." Our fellowship is unshakable and unbreakable because of the one-time sacrifice of Jesus Christ that needs no repeat (1 John 1:3, 7; Heb. 7:25).

If we're going to sin, then we sin while we're in fellowship. We sin while we're joined to Jesus Christ. We sin as we're one spirit with his Spirit and seated right next to the Father (Rom. 6:5; Phil. 2:1; 1 Cor. 6:17; Eph. 2:6). We take Father, Son, and Holy Spirit along with us when we sin. Maybe that's why it's just not as fun as it used to be. Some people lie awake at night dreaming of new ways to sin. For some reason, we continually seek to escape sin's clutches. Maybe it goes back to our new identity. New creations can afford to be totally forgiven.

New creations don't really want to sin anyway.

When we commit sins, we experience consequences. There's the reactions of others and our own lack of fulfillment. But Christ never leaves us. We are always in fellowship with him. Even when we are faithless, our God remains faithful (2 Tim. 2:13).

WATERING DOWN THE WAGES

The false idea that we Christians somehow go "in and out" of fellowship with God involves a *watering down of the wages of sin*. Remember that the wages of sin is death (Rom. 6:23), not some lesser punishment. The wages of sin is not merely a bit of God's anger expressed toward us for a day or a week. And the wages of sin is not God's face being rotated away from us for a few short minutes or hours until we get our act together.

> Our God is *not* in a swivel chair, rotating his face away when we sin.

No, the wages of sin is *death*, nothing less.

Our God is *not* in a swivel chair, rotating his face away when we sin. Because of the cross, his face is always toward us (1 Pet. 3:12). Because Jesus was forsaken on the cross, God will never forsake us (Heb. 13:5). In the work of the Son, we see the plan of a Father who desired to be with us, in us, and for us every moment of every day. From that permanent and unshakable relationship, we live life.

That's the truth about our freedom from the law of sin and death. We live life on a higher plane. The law of the Spirit of life in Christ Jesus has delivered us entirely from the law of sin and death. We can celebrate that or even abuse it (1 Cor. 6:12; 10:23), but true fulfillment only comes as we *allow grace to teach us* to say no to sin and to live the upright lives that are our destiny as children of God:

> For *the grace of God* that brings salvation has appeared to all men. *It teaches us* to say "No" to ungodliness and worldly passions, and to live self-controlled, upright and godly lives in this present age. (Titus 2:11–12)

ALL EYES ON JESUS!

If I were to challenge you to a one-mile footrace, you might win. But one way to ensure my victory would be to ask you to run backward. It's a lot more difficult to run if you can only see where you've already been, and not where you're going. Similarly, it's really hard to run the race called life if we're consumed with our past or present struggles. Professional runners not only face forward, they look way out in front of them. Often they fixate on another runner out in the distance.

The incredible, irreversible forgiveness we have in Christ enables us to look out ahead. Rather than obsessing about our own performance, we can look out ahead at someone who is not us. We can fix our eyes on our forerunner, Jesus Christ—the author and perfecter of our faith:

> This hope we have as an anchor of the soul, a hope both sure and steadfast and one which enters within the veil, *where Jesus has entered as a forerunner for us*, having become a high priest forever according to the order of Melchizedek. (Heb. 6:19–20 NASB)

> *Let us fix our eyes on Jesus*, the author and perfecter of our faith, who for the joy set before him endured the cross, scorning its shame, and sat down at the right hand of the throne of God. (Heb. 12:2)

God is calling us to a new way. We may feel it's spiritual to analyze ourselves and our sins. Maybe we think that by dwelling on our sins for a time and doing some sort of guilty penance, God will be pleased and restore us to a former state of "fellowship." But the gospel is better than all of that. The gospel invites us to dwell on the work of Jesus Christ instead. We are invited to be obsessed with the cross, not our sins.

Are you infatuated with your sins when God remembers them no more? Are you obsessed with your failures instead of God's success on the cross? Are you so consumed with your struggles that you aren't looking anywhere else except upon yourself?

The Son of Man has been lifted up. Religion would have us look at our sins. God is saying, "Look at my Son."

28

The Lord is coming back tomorrow," he said, "so it's important that you know where you stand!" When I was twelve years old, our church youth leader invited us to his house for a special meeting. It seemed he'd been doing some reading and calculating, and 1984 was the year of Christ's return. On top of that, he apparently had narrowed it down to the exact day. At the meeting, he revealed that Jesus was coming back to "get us."

As you can imagine, there were mixed reactions to that phrasing.

Some kids were excited, while others got real nervous. My reaction? Well, my mom had warned me about the evening: "Drew, if you go to youth group tonight, the leader is going to tell you that Jesus is coming back tomorrow. But I want you to know—it's *not* true."

"Um, okay, Mom," I said. What else do you say to that one?

So I weathered the storm. I sat there all evening, with trust in my mom's words, undisturbed by what I was hearing. And through stealthy whispers behind the leader's back, I was even able to rescue a few kids from their confusion. It was all because my mom knew something—she knew that *no one* can predict Christ's return (Matt. 24:36; 1 Thess. 5:2–3).

DOUBLE JEOPARDY?

What surprised me the most about that evening was how *scared* everyone was! It seems to me that if our Savior is returning, we should be celebrating, not freaking out. And apparently, I'm not the only one who thinks this. The apostle John tells us that if we have fear concerning the day of judgment, it's because we're wrongly imagining some punishment:

> In this way, love is made complete among us so that we will have *confidence on the day of judgment*, because in this world we are like him [God]. There is no fear in love. But *perfect love drives out fear*, because *fear has to do with punishment*. The one who fears is not made perfect in love. (1 John 4:17–18)

Apparently, we're supposed to be confident about the day of judgment. The reason for our confidence is that "we are like him." What does that mean? What is it about *who we are* that would free us from any fear of judgment? Our newness, our righteousness, our closeness to God—all of these contribute to our confidence on judgment day.

We are to trust in the love of God. It was God's love that sent Jesus to the cross to take away our sins forever. It was his love that brought us this incredible, unconditional forgiveness and cleansing. Do we really believe that, having done all of this, he will double-cross us upon Jesus's return, bringing up the very sins he has removed and forgotten?

There is no punishment left.

In our legal system here in the United States, this is referred to as "double jeopardy." A person cannot be tried for the same criminal offense twice. With God, it's essentially the same. We were already put on trial, and the verdict was guilty. The punishment was death, and Jesus died in our place. Now there is no punishment left, and we will never again be put on trial for our sins. If we were to be judged for our sins after Christ died for them and took them away, that'd be a case of double jeopardy. That's not happening!

> Christ also, *having been offered once* to bear the sins of many, will appear a second time for salvation *without reference to sin*, to those who eagerly await Him. (Heb. 9:28 NASB)

When Christ returns, he will return without reference to sin. Why? Because we've already been put on trial, and God carried out the sentence on his Son. As this passage says, Christ was already *offered once* for our sins, and in the eyes of God, that's enough.

There will be no double jeopardy.

BLACK-AND-WHITE THRONE JUDGMENT

The idea that we believers will face a final judgment for our sins contradicts total forgiveness. But many of us seem to think that Christians will be held accountable for their sins. Held accountable? If we were held accountable for our sins, the punishment would be death. It wouldn't be a slap on the wrist.

Remember, the wages of sin is *death*.

Yes, Paul tells us "we must *all* appear before the judgment seat of Christ" (2 Cor. 5:10). So all *humans* will appear at the judgment. But the question is, what will that judgment look like? Fortunately, other passages reveal the specifics of a black-and-white judgment that may be different from what we've imagined.

In Revelation 20, God summons "the dead" to be pulled from hell for judgment of their deeds. The result is that they're all judged guilty and then thrown into the lake of fire:

> *The sea gave up the dead* that were in it, and *death and Hades gave up the dead* that were in them, and each person was judged according to what he had done. *Then death and Hades* were thrown into the lake of fire. The lake of fire is the second death. If anyone's name was *not found written in the book of life*, he was thrown into the lake of fire. (Rev. 20:13–15)

It's a black-and-white, pass-fail judgment, and they fail. Their final destination is what's at stake. And they all receive the same verdict—the lake of fire.

The next verses in Revelation 21 are very different. God has already completed his judgment of "the dead." He then addresses *the church*. As you'll read, he's got nothing but positive things to say to his bride as he assures us there'll be no sadness of any kind for us:

Then I saw a new heaven and a new earth, for the first heaven and the first earth had passed away, and there was no longer any sea. I saw the Holy City, the new Jerusalem, coming down out of heaven from God, *pre-pared as a bride beautifully dressed for her husband.* And I heard a loud voice from the throne saying, "Now the dwelling of God is with men, and he will live with them. They will be his people, and God himself will be with them and be their God. *He will wipe every tear from their eyes. There will be no more death or mourning or crying or pain, for the old order of things has passed away."* (Rev. 21:1–4)

There's no movie to be played.

So why don't Christians go through a Revelation 20 judgment for our sins? Simple. We aren't hell bound! Our sins are forgiven, and our sins are forgotten. We show up later in Revelation 21, and our names are in the book of life. I guess God really means what he says:

"He who believes in Him *is not judged.*" (John 3:18 NASB)

If we're experiencing fear about Christ's return, it may be that religion has told us there'll be a heavenly movie reel of our sins spinning as everyone watches. And when the movie is over, we're going to pay, big-time. But the reality is that there's no movie to be played.

In his love, God destroyed the reel.

WE'RE SHEEP, NOT GOATS!

Jesus's parable about the sheep and goats in Matthew 25 also depicts a black-and-white judgment with a black-and-white result. Jesus tells the story of sheep that hear his voice, and they're praised even for giving a cup of water in his name. Apparently, even the smallest act done in his name is an expression of him. On the other hand, the goats do not hear his voice, and they're eternally condemned. Notice that there are *only two distinct groups*. There's no gray area. Again, it's black and white:

> When the Son of Man comes in his glory, and all the angels with him, he will sit on his throne in heavenly glory. All the nations will be gathered before him, and he will *separate the people one from another* as a shepherd separates the sheep from the goats. He will put the *sheep on his right* and the *goats on his left*. (Matt. 25:31–33)

In the verses that follow, the *sheep* are told to "take your inheritance" and enjoy "the kingdom prepared for you" (v. 34). They are referred to as "the righteous" (v. 37). Conversely, Jesus teaches that God will then "say to those on his left, 'Depart from me, you who are cursed, into the eternal fire prepared for the devil and his angels'" (v. 41). Not only are there two distinct groups, there are two distinct results to this judgment. And there's no middle ground.

Jesus sums up all the events in this way: "Then they [the cursed] will go away to *eternal punishment*, but the righteous to *eternal life*" (v. 46). Do you see it? The black-and-white truth is that Christians will not be judged for their sins. We're the sheep! If we were judged for our sins, we'd have to be thrown into hell with the goats. No lesser punishment for sins will do.

Jesus died so that we'd be forgiven, so that our sins would be forgotten (yes, forgotten!), and so that we'd never face judgment for them.

Now that's truth that sets you free!

THE MR. T STARTER SET

"But we're still going to receive fewer rewards if we don't do a lot of good works, right?" some will ask. The rewards theology has led some to expect that there's a heavenly point system. Our performance here on earth leads to different quantities or qualities of rewards being doled out, we might think.

For many, it's all about jewelry. Some believe they'll have to settle for the "Mr. T Starter Set," while their more committed friends will receive the deluxe "Ultra Bling Kit." (Note that some televangelists have already received this kit in advance.) Or maybe some will get only one crown, while others will get multiple crowns and have to stack them. Or we may only get one crown each, but some of us are going to get a serious neck workout since our crowns will be weighted down with so many mega-sized gems. Or maybe it all comes down to square footage—some of us will enjoy an estate in Beverly Heavens, while others are resigned to living in One-Story Purgatory across the tracks. Those are the ones who became Christians later in life or just did a whole lot of misbehaving.

This is how the rewards theology goes, more or less.

There's only one problem with all of this—it's just not true. The word *rewards* (plural) is absent from any New

Testament letter. The Epistles tell us there's a reward (singular), a prize (singular), a crown of life (singular)—all seeming to refer to the same thing: eternal life with Jesus. This is very different from the idea that we are collecting Divine Dollars to fund our mansion expansion.

GOD: AN EQUAL OPPORTUNITY EMPLOYER

In Matthew 20, Jesus tells the story of a landowner who went out early in the morning to hire men to work in his vineyard. He agreed to pay each of them a denarius and sent them off to work. About the third hour, he saw others and hired them. About the sixth hour and the ninth hour, he hired some more. Then, even at the eleventh hour, he hired more workers.

The word *rewards* (plural) is absent from any New Testament letter.

When evening came, the foreman called all the workers together to pay them. The workers hired at the last minute were paid first— one denarius. When the others saw this, you can imagine what they thought: "We're really going to score!" But it turns out that all the workers got paid the same, regardless of when they started. Those who had been working since early in the morning started grumbling, "This isn't fair! We've been working all day!" Then the landowner fired back, "Don't I have the right to do what I want with my own money?" (v. 15).

Jesus's parable is a picture of the kingdom of God—we all get paid the same. So why are we adding an *s* to the biblical word *reward* and then going through life trying to collect tokens for Heaven's Gift Shop? Paul reminds us that everything is absolutely dung next to knowing Jesus (Phil. 3:8). If that's true, why do we expect the "reward," the "prize," the "crown of life" to be anything other than *knowing him*?

Religion tells us we'll be *judged* for our sins and *collect rewards* for our good deeds. God tells us that Jesus was punished for our sins and that knowing Jesus himself is our great reward. One idea leads to walking on eggshells and doing good things to collect heavenly loot. The other idea leads to gratefulness for God's grace and a new ambition in life—to know Jesus.

Which do *you* believe is the truth that sets us free?

29

Okay, maybe we Christians aren't judged after we die, but God still punishes us with *earthly* consequences, doesn't he?"

To discuss this one, I'd like to take you to the theater.

A Day at Ragtown

Chip and Glenn Polk founded Ragtown Gospel Theater in Post, Texas. Chip is a gifted playwright, and his brother Glenn is an incredible actor. They're the perfect duo to operate a world-class theater. During their first year, Glenn was the one and only actor, and he put on incredible individual performances as Peter the Rock, Judas Iscariot, and other characters. But as the years went by, Chip decided to start writing more complex works that required elaborate sets and additional cast members.

Imagine I invite you to Ragtown Gospel Theater for one of their performances. Let's say there are five or six main actors, and the play is called *Magdalene*. After the roar of applause, the standing ovation, and the drop of the final curtain, I ask you what you thought of the performance.

"Glenn was fantastic!" you exclaim.

"He sure was! What'd you think of the girl who played Magdalene?" I ask.

Looking a bit confused, you reply, "Yeah, that Glenn sure is an incredible actor."

Now puzzled myself, I ask, "But what did you think of the *other* actors?"

"What other actors?" you respond in a surprised tone. "I didn't see any others."

THEATER OF LIFE

I paint this silly scenario to make a point about how we Christians can go through life attributing *everything* to God, the Master Thespian. But not everything we see should be attributed to his actions.

There are *other* actors in the theater of life.

Although it's simplest to blame God for everything that hits us, it's important to recognize the roles played by other actors—the world, the flesh, and the devil. It's especially important if we're going to get our belief system straight about the Christian's freedom from judgment and punishment.

A Christian gets sick. Then he loses his job. Then his wife divorces him. Then his friends start trying to connect the dots to find out why God did this to him. Sound like any story you've heard before? Yeah, it's the book of Job all over again. And today we're still quick to put the God stamp on *everything* that happens to us.

God doesn't want the credit. A drunk driver rams into a friend's car at the intersection, and a two-year-old girl dies in the backseat. "Well, the Lord took her," some might say.

I know God is sovereign. But I also know that God wasn't drunk that day, and God didn't steer the car into that little girl's way. No, we can chalk that one up to the other actors in the theater of life. The world teaches us overindulgence is okay. The flesh craves alcohol to drown our sorrows. We are tempted to go ahead and drive drunk because "It's no big deal."

God doesn't want the credit. God *allowed* that circumstance, but he didn't *cause* it. That's important to differentiate. God never treats us cruelly. He does not inflict wounds on his own children. But as a loving Father, *he comforts and helps us in the midst of earthly turmoil.* And we come out on the other side with a better understanding of his relentless love for us:

> And we know that *in all things God works for the good* of those who love him, who have been called according to his purpose. For those God foreknew he also predestined *to be conformed to the likeness of his Son*, that he might be the firstborn among many brothers. (Rom. 8:28–29)

God is not the author of all things—sin, pain, death. But God uses *all things* of this world as a training ground to enable us to grow in our reflection of the character of Jesus Christ. All Christians have been destined for that privilege—to exude the glory of Christ, whether on this earth or in the world to come. No, God is not the author of our pain. But he is "the author and perfecter of our *faith*" (Heb. 12:2).

WHEN DISASTER STRIKES

Some preachers have claimed God brought the 9/11 terrorist attacks on New York City to teach homosexuals a lesson. Several years later, others said God brought Hurricane Katrina on New Orleans to punish the city for debauchery. Still others even had the audacity to say the 2010 earthquake in Haiti was retribution for deals made with the devil.

I hope these statements sound absurd to you. But the reality is that *many* of us subtly equate our negative circumstances with punishment from God. A smoker we know gets lung cancer, and you might hear a Christian remark, "Well, that's God's way of getting his attention." Or some might say it in a more spiritual sounding way: "God is bringing this on him to make him into a broken man."

Essentially, we're believing that injury, illness, and negative circumstances on earth are delivered to us by the hand of God as punishment for our sins. Now, whether it's cancer, terrorism, or natural disaster, I want to state very clearly the following: *those are not brought upon us as punishment from God for our sins.* How can I be so sure? Because all punishment for our sins was placed on Jesus Christ at the cross. Today, on this side of the cross, God is in the business of saving people on planet earth, not punishing them:

For I did not come to judge the world, but *to save it*. (John 12:47)

The Lord is not slow in keeping his promise, as some understand slowness. He is patient with you, *not wanting anyone to perish, but everyone to come to repentance.* (2 Peter 3:9)

There'll be a day when Christ returns and God judges the world (John 12:48). But for right now, the Son of Man has been lifted up, and he is drawing all men unto himself (John 12:32). God doesn't want anyone to **God is not killing** be punished but wants all to believe in Jesus **people through** Christ for salvation (2 Pet. 3:9). **terrorism or** So God is not killing people through ter- **natural disasters.** rorism or natural disasters; nor is he bringing disease upon them to teach them a lesson. Instead, it's his desire that the world look upon his Son, the full payment for their sins:

God was in Christ *reconciling the world* to Himself, *not counting their trespasses against them*, and He has committed to us the word of reconciliation. (2 Cor. 5:19 NASB)

He Himself is the propitiation for our sins; and not for ours only, but also for those of *the whole world*. (1 John 2:2 NASB)

The message we have for the world is *not* that God is punishing them with this or that. No, God was in Christ "reconciling the *world* to himself" (2 Cor. 5:19). The punishment for the sins "of the *whole world*" was paid in full

(1 John 2:2). Here's what the Lord himself says he wants for the world:

> To *open their eyes* and turn them from darkness to light, and from the power of Satan to God, *so that they may receive forgiveness of sins* and a place among those who are sanctified by faith in me. (Acts 26:18)

WHEN CONSEQUENCES HIT

That's not to say there aren't consequences for our actions. For example, there's no question that scientific research has shown a strong correlation between smoking and the likelihood of contracting lung cancer. Without a doubt, a smoker takes on a great risk by inhaling smoke into his lungs on a daily basis.

And there are all kinds of earthly consequences for our risky or foolish choices. In fact, it's just as risky to eat fast food frequently as it is to smoke. Have you ever noticed that pastors can be very good at preaching against smoking (and drinking)? Yet at the same time studies have shown that we ministers tend to be some of the more obese people in America!

There are all kinds of choices—health choices, lifestyle choices, morality choices—and each choice carries a certain risk. Rather than insinuating that certain choices bring punishment from God, we should teach the cross as sufficient punishment for all sins. Sure, we should warn other believers about the consequences of their actions—health concerns, broken relationships, trouble with the law, or personal ruin. But let's not call those "punishment from God."

With regard to punishment, it is finished.

GOD'S DISCIPLINE

Even though God doesn't punish us, doesn't he *discipline* us? Yes, Hebrews talks about the discipline that we experience as children of God:

> And you have forgotten the exhortation which is addressed to you as sons: "My son, do not regard lightly the discipline of the Lord, nor faint when you are reproved by Him. For those whom the Lord loves He disciplines, and *He scourges every son whom He receives.*" (Heb. 12:5–6 NASB)

Wait, rewind. Scourges? That's the act of beating someone on the back with a long strip of leather that has shards of sharp metal embedded in it. The metal digs into the person's back and leaves open wounds that can, if left untreated, kill the person. This is precisely what the Roman soldiers did to Jesus before he was taken to the cross to be crucified. If you've seen Mel Gibson's *The Passion of the Christ*, you know exactly how to picture it. This is *not* what most parents of the day did to their disobedient children. After all, it could kill them!

Is this how God treats *us* as his children?

First, it's important to note that the phrase "and He scourges every son whom He receives" (Heb. 12:6 NASB) was added to the Proverbs 3:12 quote. It does *not* appear in the Old Testament passage. Even more interesting, there's a Hebrew term *biqqoret* that can mean "to scourge" or "to inquire into." And the "inquire" meaning is older than the "scourge" meaning, as the scourging weapon was invented much later. Is it possible that Hebrews was originally written in Hebrew and that *biqqoret* (also meaning "to inquire into") originally appeared in this controversial verse?

The early church scholar Clement (ca. 150–215) and others believed that Hebrews was written in Hebrew and later translated into Greek. Interestingly, more than 150 words used in Hebrews don't appear in any other epistles. In fact, some expressions aren't found in biblical or classical Greek at all. On top of that, the epistle's literary characteristics mirror Hebrew poetry at times. So either Hebrews as a whole or just the altered Old Testament quote in verse 6 may have been written in Hebrew and later translated to Greek. This would mean that the original author used the Hebrew word *biqqoret*, a word translatable as "scourge" (*mastigoo*) in Greek. It would also mean the translator didn't consider or perhaps showed bias against the older meaning of *biqqoret*, which is "to inquire into."

So there is both historical and literary evidence that the epistle (or just the altered Old Testament quote) may have been written in Hebrew and later mistranslated using the expression "scourge" (Greek: *mastigoo*) in verse 6. Coincidentally, the Hebrew word *biqqoret* stems from *baqar*, meaning "to plow." And the writer of Hebrews goes on to say that God's discipline "produces *a harvest* of righteousness and peace for those who have been trained by it" (v. 11). Essentially, Hebrews 12 may be conveying this: *God deeply inquires into our lives as he disciplines us, so that we can experience a harvest of righteousness and peace.*

God cares about our behavior. He cares about our future. So he deeply inquires into our lives and lovingly disciplines us toward maturity. But it's equally important to remember that Jesus was scourged two thousand years ago.

And "by *His* stripes we are healed" (Isa. 53:5 NKJV).

HARDSHIP AS DISCIPLINE

A common misconception is that God disciplines us *only when we sin*. This is not the picture painted here in Hebrews 12:

> Endure *hardship as discipline*; God is treating you as sons. For what son is not disciplined by his father? (v. 7)

We're *always* under the discipline of the Lord as he uses our good times and our hardships to show us his ways. It's not that the Hebrew believers were sinning and then God reacted. No, they were being persecuted for their faith, enduring incredible hardship. This passage was written to comfort them, encourage them, and tell them they were on the right road. God's discipline gave them a sense of purpose in the midst of all the turmoil. They learned that God's discipline is training for the future, not punishment for the past.

God's discipline is training for the future, not punishment for the past.

Trials and hardships are the means by which we grow in Christ. During the most difficult circumstances imaginable, we are privileged to have God's active participation in our lives:

> No discipline seems pleasant at the time, but painful. Later on, however, it produces a harvest of righteousness and peace for those who have been trained by it. (Heb. 12:11)

God tells human fathers to "not exasperate your children; instead, bring them up in the training and instruction *of the Lord*" (Eph. 6:4). Apparently, our Father's form of training and instruction does not exasperate us. Think of the most loving human father you can imagine, and then ask yourself: How much *more* loving is my heavenly Dad? Apparently, that's what this writer would have us do!

> Moreover, *we have all had human fathers who disciplined us* and we respected them for it. How much more should we submit to the Father of our spirits and live! Our fathers disciplined us for a little while as they thought best; but *God disciplines us for our good*, that we may share in his holiness. (Heb. 12:9–10)

30

The security guard bolted out of his office and stood in the middle of my lane, signaling for me to stop. And the police officer was catching up to me from behind. What could I do? Nothing. I was busted, and I'd had it coming for months.

I was seventeen years old, and it was my first year away from home at university. I'd been out with friends that night, entertaining a prospective student. She was attractive, and I was all about showing off. So I invited her to ride back to campus with me after a group of us had been out at the International House of Pancakes. (That's the Christian version of college partying.)

I was going about eight or ten miles per hour over the speed limit when I saw the blue lights flashing in my rear-view mirror. My desire to show off and to avoid a speeding ticket gave way to a moment of severe indiscretion.

I stomped on the gas pedal and took off.

We exceeded speeds of 140 miles per hour for over three miles before I reached the university campus. As I screeched around the exit ramp toward the university entrance, the security guard heard me coming. That's why he stood in the road, foiling my getaway. The police were only a half mile behind me and caught up easily when I had to stop at the front gate.

Within seconds, I was pulled from my car and handcuffed. "Why'd you run, son?" the officer asked. "You weren't even going that fast when I turned on my lights. I probably would've just given you a warning and let you off."

My seventeen-year-old mind froze up in disbelief at my own stupidity. "Uh, I don't know, sir!"

Just then, my friends pulled up in their own car only to watch me get escorted to the squad car and hauled away. From there, I spent a night in jail and faced other sobering consequences—a major fine and suspension of my license. Oh, and the girl? Her parents encouraged her to pick *another* college.

"Mom, Dad, I did something really stupid."

This happened only a few days before fall break, so I had to go home to Virginia and face my parents right after. I was petrified at the thought of telling them what I'd done, but I knew I had to. All the way home I rehearsed what I'd say.

When I got home, it was already getting late. And there were lots of reasons I could've waited until morning. But I had to get it over with. I walked right into their bedroom, sat down at the foot of their bed, and let it fly.

"Mom, Dad, I did something really stupid. I ran from a police officer when he tried to pull me over. Not only did I run, but I was going really fast, and I put someone else's life at risk. The officer caught up to me, and I spent a night in jail." After getting it all out, I broke down crying because of the shame. I was only seventeen, and I'd never been to jail before. Nothing even close. What would my parents say? How would they react?

After my dad recovered from a moment of shock, he asked, "Are you all right, son? Did you get hurt?" My mother sat listening, tears of concern streaming down her cheeks. I sat there in disbelief as my parents overwhelmed me with their heartfelt concern. Never in any of my rehearsals did it go like this. Where was the yelling? The lecture? There was no sermon, not even a hint of anger. I guess they thought I'd already been through enough and that adding to my consequences wouldn't really help.

I'm no expert on parenting, but I will say the approach my parents took in those circumstances was life changing for me. It's been over twenty years since that conversation, and I won't forget it for the rest of my life. God used it to imprint on my mind a snapshot of the true meaning of grace. I was able to see how a parent might choose concern over anger, even when a very serious sin had been committed. No, I'm not recommending we get our view of God from our parents. But if, in that moment, my parents could choose concern over anger, I thought, *how much more could God do so, all the time?*

Saints in the Arms of a Loving God

It's not that God didn't get angry at sin. He got very angry. And it's not as if there was no punishment for sin. There was, and it was the ultimate punishment: death and separation from God. So this isn't just cheap grace talk. The loving, grace-filled attitude that God has for us *all the time*, even when we sin, is due to one very expensive reason: Jesus became sin for us and absorbed all the punishment we deserved:

> God made him who had no sin *to be sin for us*, so that in him *we might become the righteousness of God.* (2 Cor. 5:21)

> *He himself bore our sins* in his body on the tree, so that we might die to sins and live for righteousness; by his wounds you have been healed. (1 Pet. 2:24)

> But he was pierced for *our* transgressions,
>   he was crushed for *our* iniquities;
> *the punishment that brought us peace was upon*
>   *him,*
>   and by his wounds we are healed. (Isa. 53:5)

Every ounce of God's anger and every gram of the punishment for those sins was put on his Son. The result of Jesus's death and resurrection is that we became the righteousness of God! None of God's anger remains for us. After all, *how angry is God with his own righteousness?* As Paul tells us in Romans, we are *saved* from the wrath of God (Rom. 5:9). John also tells us that "perfect love drives out fear, because *fear has to do with punishment*. The one who fears is not made perfect in love" (1 John 4:18).

Many from the time of Jonathan Edwards until now have been impacted by this early American's dynamic sermons. Edwards's most recognized sermon is his "Sinners in the

Hands of an Angry God." But in light of what we've seen, is it really accurate to think of us *Christians* in that way?

Are *we* sinners in the hands of an angry God?

We are saints in the arms of a loving God. It makes no sense to claim Jesus as our satisfying sacrifice for sins and then believe in an angry God, a God who still has punishment in store for us as recompense for our sins. No, instead of being "sinners in the hands of an angry God," we are *saints in the arms of a loving God*.

THE TIGER WOODS AFFAIR

On November 25, 2009, reports began surfacing that Tiger Woods, the greatest golfer in the world, was having an affair. Shortly thereafter, Tiger was found at the scene of a car accident just outside his Orlando home. His Cadillac Escalade had collided with a fire hydrant and then a tree. Emergency vehicles rushed to the scene and carried Tiger away. Early police reports indicated that Tiger's wife had smashed the rear window in an attempt to pull Tiger to safety. Later it was alleged that she had actually broken the rear window during a domestic dispute with Tiger.

It's unlikely that any of us will ever know the details of what happened that night. But one thing we can be sure of—this was the beginning of a very stressful period in the life of Tiger Woods.

Things got worse from there as Tiger's numerous affairs became public. These events led to Tiger losing sponsors and fans and going through a heartbreaking divorce. Eventually he would return to the game of golf, but not before months of counseling and treatment for what was termed "a sexual addiction." Tiger experienced public humiliation, a lengthy hiatus from the profession he loves, and major damage to his personal life.

When asked about Tiger's behavior, Tiger's caddy, Steve Williams, had this to say:

> When you're a true friend of somebody, that's when somebody needs your support and needs you the most. That's when you don't walk away. Tiger's one of my closest friends and he needs my support right now, and I'd never think of walking away. When I talk to him, I don't talk to him about what's happened. I talk to him about the future and about what we're going to try to accomplish and how we're going to get over it.*

Mr. Williams apparently knows something of grace. And he chose grace when it mattered most. Sure, Tiger has committed heinous acts, but he has also paid dearly for those, publicly and privately. It appears that his caddy recognized this and decided to play the role of a loyal friend, comforter, and encourager.

Tiger was already remorseful. Would it have done him any good for Williams to point a finger in Tiger's face and tell him how ashamed he ought to be? Williams chose differently. Did you catch what he said? "I'd never think of walking away," and "I talk to him about the future," and about "how we're going to get over it."

*Steve Williams, interview by Karen McCarthy, "Tiger Woods: In the Rough," *60 Minutes* video, 3 News (Wellington, New Zealand), March 4, 2010, http://www.3news.co.nz/Video/60Minutes/tabid/371/articleID/144663/Default.aspx.

If a friend can be this gracious in circumstances this bad, how much more is our Father inviting us to "approach the throne of grace with confidence, so that we may receive *mercy* and find *grace* to help us in our time of need" (Heb. 4:16). Yes, we quickly nod our heads that God is good. But realizing that God is "good *to me*" is an entirely different thought. And actually believing that God is "good to me *all the time*" is absolutely life changing. It's not about religion. It's about family ties to a supportive Father that are stronger than we can possibly imagine:

> Both the one who makes men holy and those who are made holy are of *the same family*. So Jesus is not ashamed to call them brothers. (Heb. 2:11)

> How great is *the love the Father has lavished on us*, that we should be called children of God! And that is what we are! (1 John 3:1)

PART 8

THE SPIRIT OF GRETZKY

> To be in Christ—that makes you fit
> for heaven; but for Christ to be in
> you—that makes you fit for earth!
> Major Ian Thomas (1914–2007)

31

Around the time I was born, there was a nationwide evangelistic campaign going on in churches across America. At my parents' church, the pastor and his wife were forming and leading training groups to help people share their faith. The pastor and his wife would go from group to group and model how to present the gospel as everyone observed and learned. Then the group members would practice delivering their testimonies and asking the listener if they'd like to make a decision to receive Christ.

The pastor's wife decided it might be more efficient to *record* her delivery of the gospel and distribute cassette tapes around the church. That way, the whole congregation would have an opportunity to get trained without attending meetings. So she recorded her personalized version of "the plan of salvation" and distributed the tapes to everyone around her. And her training tapes were having quite an impact, helping church members become confident in their own delivery of the gospel.

One day, while driving down the road in her van, she decided to pop the tape in the cassette deck and listen to the example she'd prepared. Much to her surprise, those same old words she'd said hundreds of times suddenly sounded very different, even new. By the time the recording ended, tears were streaming down her cheeks. She pulled to the roadside, and right there and then she received Jesus as her personal Savior.

Yes, she led *herself* to Christ! It was through her own voice sharing the gospel message that she came to know Jesus.

I tell you this true story to make an important point. Sometimes we think we know the gospel, when all we really know is religion. It's very possible to have Christian religion *without* God. We may find ourselves saying all the right things and using all the right terminology about a spiritual matter. But in the end, it is only when we are open to the beauty of grace that we'll really learn. And, strangely, as the pastor's wife found out, God can even use our own words!

So what did the pastor's wife have before she "led herself to salvation"? She certainly had a very Christian-looking, morally upright, and, many would have thought, even Spirit-filled life. She thought it was important that everyone know about Jesus; she'd thrown herself into the church's evangelistic campaign; she supported her husband, helped in the church, led Bible studies, and in general looked just like any other pastor's wife, maybe even a bit better than most. But she accomplished all of that without having the life of Christ in her.

She had religion, but no *life*.

His Best Life Now!

The true meaning of *eternal* life offers incredible insight into what it really means to be saved. For years I thought "eternal" and "everlasting" were synonyms meaning the same thing. But "everlasting" is only *half* of the meaning of "eternal." Sure, eternal life lasts forever. But eternal life also has *no beginning*. Eternal life, by definition, means life with no beginning and no end.

So if we have eternal life, whose life do we possess?

Our own lives had a beginning. I was born on October 31, 1972. That's when my life began. But now I'm a possessor of eternal life—a life that has no beginning and no end. So what life, or whose life, do I possess? Having eternal life means *possessing God's divine life.*

Eternal life is not your life made better. Eternal life is not your life made longer. Eternal life is an altogether different life—a life not your own now imparted to you. Eternal life is Christ's life:

> **Eternal life is not your life made longer.**

Because I live, you also will live. (John 14:19)

When *Christ, who is your life*, appears, then you also will appear with him in glory. (Col. 3:4)

True Christianity isn't just a ticket to heaven. Nor does it primarily involve studying a religious book. Nor is it centrally about reforming one's attitudes and actions. Although heaven, the Bible, and behavior play an important role, they're not the primary reason that Christ died and rose again. Jesus said plainly, "I have come that they may *have life* and have it *to the full*" (John 10:10).

Real salvation is possessing Christ's life within our physical shell. This means that here and now, we participate in God's divine nature (2 Pet. 1:4). The life once lost in Eden is now restored to us through Christ Jesus. Christ's *death* reconciled us to God. But it's actually Christ's resurrection *life* that saves us!

> If, when we were God's enemies, we were *reconciled to him through the death* of his Son, how much more, having been reconciled, shall we be *saved through his life*! (Rom. 5:10)

REDIRECTING PLEASANTVILLE

In the Hollywood film *Pleasantville*, all the residents of the town are living life in black and white until one day someone discovers the forbidden idea of free choice. Upon making that choice, the main character turns into a vibrant, colorful person while everyone else remains black and white. From there, other citizens of Pleasantville discover free choice, and they too exchange their black-and-white existence for dynamic color.

One message we might take away from this film is that it's those who choose freely the life of sin and fleshly fulfillment who are living life in color, while all others are doomed to a grayscale existence. This is precisely the view of sin that the enemy would love for us to buy into. Ever found yourself asking, "Why is the world getting away with murder, while I as a Christian am supposed to live uprightly?" In other words, why does the world get to experience the Technicolor dream life while I'm stuck with this black-and-white existence?

The truth is, that's backward. We might picture sin dangling in front of our eyes as the most fulfilling thing out there and think it's our obligation to resist it simply because God says not to partake. But that's a distorted view of the spiritual reality. The reality is that we are now partakers of God's divine nature. We're the ones who can experience life in vibrant, heavenly color.

An unbeliever can only choose one thing—sin. It may be good-looking sin, philanthropic sin, or kind and compassionate sin. But if it's not an expression of the life of Christ, then it's still *sin*. It's a black-and-white expression of death rather than the life of Christ in dynamic color.

> We are now partakers of God's divine nature.

We Christians can also choose sin. But we'll find, over and over, that it never fulfills. We're simply not made for it anymore. We've been redesigned from the ground up as a people in God's living color so that we can display and transmit *his* life in this world.

Life for us is like the film *Pleasantville* but rewritten, redirected. God has the market cornered on fulfillment. As his children, we're the only ones who can live the Technicolor dream. Interestingly, not only do we look different, apparently we even *smell* different:

> For *we are to God the aroma of Christ* among those who are being saved and those who are perishing. (2 Cor. 2:15)

32

My wife loves to watch TV shows about dancing. One of her favorites is *Dancing with the Stars*. Every season the show likes to push the envelope with a variety of dancers, from the very young to the very old. But one season they dished out the biggest challenge ever: they invited Marlee Matlin to join the cast.

Deaf since she was a toddler, Marlee has overcome her childhood condition to become highly successful, the youngest person ever to win an Academy Award for best actress. But still—acting is one thing, dancing is another. To dance, you have to move in time to the music, music that Marlee can't hear. Her professional dance partner was up to the task, though. From getting Marlee to stand on his feet while they were dancing, to tapping out the beat with his hands, he made sure Marlee was on time and in sync to the music.

Marlee did an amazing job! If you didn't know she was deaf and just happened to turn to that channel while she was dancing, you wouldn't have noticed anything out of the ordinary. But still, no matter how good it looked, what she was doing was simply imitating her partner's timing. Her partner could hear the music and move in time to it; but all Marlee had was a vague beat that she could sometimes feel but not really hear. Marlee was forced to obsess about her partner and his every move. Without imitating him, she'd be lost!

Compare Marlee to any other celebrity contestant on the program. While none of them were professional dancers, they all had their hearing. Even without their partners, they could move in time to the music (well, most of them). This is like the difference between us merely following external religious conventions versus dancing to the Spirit and his music. We might seem the same as everyone else, but we're secret Marlees—dancing in time to music we can't really hear. We carefully observe what everyone around us is doing and imitate them to the utmost of our ability.

No, I'm not talking about salvation. I'm talking about the steps we take *after* being saved. It's all too easy to forget where the "music" is coming from. We slip back into old ways of getting guidance on how to live: the Ten Commandments, so-called "Christian principles," our family values and traditions, or even just those around us. In doing so, we stop dancing in time to the music. We turn into imitators modeling ourselves after externals rather than new creations listening intently to the music that God's Spirit is playing in our hearts.

THE TEACHER WITHIN

Every religion of the world has a founder, a teacher, and therefore some teachings. If we think of Jesus as a man, or even the God-man, who lived and died and taught some wonderful things, we will proceed with our Christianity as if it were a religion. We will look back on the founder, the teacher, and the teachings and will seek to imitate and obey. We commit ourselves to a teacher from the past.

The spiritual life we carry within us is the Teacher himself. The resurrection means that the spiritual life we carry within us is the Teacher himself, the risen Christ who is seated at God's right hand. Because we are in him and he is in us, we too are seated at God's right hand. We're not part of a religion that requires us to look back and imitate a historical figure. Instead, we look within our own hearts, where Jesus literally resides today, and allow him to express himself in and through us, right here, right now.

Yes, it's the same Jesus Christ from two thousand years ago. But through the resurrection we have been admitted not just into heaven but also into a life that changes the substance of our being. We're now married to Jesus Christ, spiritually joined to him forever:

> Therefore, my brethren, you also were made to die to the Law through the body of Christ, so that you might be *joined to another, to Him who was raised* from the dead, in order that we might bear fruit for God. (Rom. 7:4 NASB)

CHRIST AS LIFE

But how do we think of it? Is it all of Christ and none of me? Is it "let go and let God"? Do I get out of the way so that he can act apart from me?

No, the gospel is greater than all of that. The new covenant message is inclusive. God is not seeking to replace us (he already has!) but instead to embrace us, since we are now new creations compatible with his nature. He desires to work *through* the uniqueness of our soul, not stomp it out or have it step aside.

This is where the rubber meets the road when it comes to God's acceptance. Do I believe that God so fully embraces every aspect of my being that he can work through my hobbies, interests, personality, and sense of humor? Do I see my *entire* self as being righteous, clean, and acceptable? Or do I merely believe those things to be some "spiritual" part of me that is far off and irrelevant, not really me? If the latter, then my gospel is no good to me in the practical moments of every day.

For the gospel to act powerfully in my life, I must believe that what Christ has done in making me new pertains to the real me who wakes up every day and lives a normal life. Then I've begun to understand my personal union with Jesus Christ. Jesus lived thirty-three years in authentic human flesh to show that his divinity is compatible with our humanity. And his divinity is entirely compatible with *your* humanity.

Christ is now my "life" (Col. 3:4), and for me, "to live is Christ" (Phil. 1:21). This is very different from Christ being a part of my life or saying that I'm going to make

Christ a priority. Saying "Christ is my life" insinuates that he permeates my being; he is the very essence of my new-found spirituality. There is an intimacy herein that no single statement on planet earth can fully capture, but Paul puts it this way:

> I have been crucified with Christ and I no longer live, but Christ lives in me. The life I live in the body, I live by faith in the Son of God, who loved me and gave himself for me. (Gal. 2:20)

Paul says he no longer lives, but then he says he *does* now live, by faith. So which is it? Does he live or doesn't he? Well, both. The old Paul (Saul of Tarsus) no longer lives, and it's now *Christ living in him*. But it's also the new Paul living in dependency on Christ.

It's a union, a mystery. And it is beautiful!

How close is *your* Jesus?

THE GREAT ONE

Wayne Gretzky, often called "the Great One," is regarded by most as the best hockey player of all time. When Gretzky retired, he held forty regular season records, fifteen playoff records, and six All-Star records. In all, Gretzky was awarded nine trophies as most valuable player, ten trophies for most points in a season, five trophies for sportsmanship, and two trophies as playoff MVP. After retiring in 1999, Gretzky was almost immediately inducted into the Hall of Fame.

What made Wayne Gretzky so great? He seemed to have a sixth sense of where everyone was on the ice and where the puck was at all times. He could weave around players like they weren't even there. He'd anticipate their moves, dodge their checks, and skate around them before they even realized it. Gretzky possessed an instinctive understanding of the game and the limits of his fellow players. And the Great One had a way all his own.

Now imagine that by some strange turn of events, you're invited to play in an NHL playoff game. Even stranger, prior to the game you find yourself inhabited by the spirit of the Great One. Yeah, the spirit of Wayne Gretzky literally indwells you. As you step out on the ice for that game, you have a choice: to play hockey like you've always played (or not played!) or depend on Gretzky to play the game through you by faith. So what will you do? You can skate to the best of your ability or allow Gretzky to motivate and animate your every move so you end up skating in a way you've never known.

It's a union, a mystery. And it is beautiful!

It's the same for those of us indwelt by the Spirit of Jesus Christ. We were never intended to live this life in our own resources or by our own methods. The entire reason we are given Jesus himself, rather than a ticket to heaven, is so that he can motivate us and animate us, living *his* life in and through us—a life we could never live apart from him.

And his divine life in us sure makes "the game" a lot more fun.

33

I took a religion course my senior year of university. At the time, I was in the midst of recovering from my own ruthless religion. So I approached the course with a desperate dependence on Christ to protect my mind from error. My goal was to complete the course unscathed.

For our final paper, the professor assigned one New Testament topic to each of us. I received "God the Father." At twenty-one years old, I was absolutely petrified of writing and presenting a paper on God. So I went home and immediately began preparing.

For weeks I researched what the New Testament had to say about God the Father. I found myself clinging to every verse I could find. I was also dumping any preconceived notions I had been holding on to. When it finally came time to write my paper, I was so afraid of going wrong that I literally put a Scripture verse in parentheses after each sentence. I didn't dare say a thing that wasn't virtually a direct quote from the Bible. I wanted to meticulously document every ounce of what I wrote.

But the night before I presented my paper, I got cold feet about all those references after every sentence. I was afraid it'd look a bit hokey and insecure. So I pulled the verses out and placed them at the very end of the paper as endnotes.

The next day, I stood up and read my paper on "God the Father." Now, remember that every sentence was a summary of Scripture that I'd found somewhere in the New Testament. I'd woven the thoughts together to present a big picture of our Father. Once I finished reading my paper aloud to the class, it was time for their comments.

> "Your God is just too good to be true."

"Your God is just too good to be true," one person said.

"Yeah, this is a God of your own invention!" another exclaimed.

That day the religion class unanimously concluded that although I had presented a kind, loving, and forgiving Father, there was no way that such a God could exist. They said I had ignored the other half of the Father's treatment of Christians—the angry God who needed justice.

I absorbed the comments and said nothing in response. I didn't even direct them to the endnotes with all the verses. I guess I lacked the confidence to confront them with what I had found in Scripture. But I *knew* what I had presented was true, even though the religion class rejected it.

GOD IS NICE

That's the irony of God without religion: when we drop all our human notions about God the Father and look to Scripture for what is *actually* true of him, we end up with a God who is "unbelievable" and "too good to be true" in the eyes of the religious world. Nevertheless, this *is* our Father—a loving, forgiving, and patient God.

"But those are all ancient 'Bible words,' and it's just hard for those words to penetrate my heart to where they're life changing," some might think. Fair enough. So how about we try some other words?

- God is *friendly* to me.
- God is *nice* to me.
- God is *encouraging* to me.
- God is *supportive* of me.
- God is *already in my corner*, every single time.

So do any of *these* help? "Well, yeah, but that's not really what the Bible says, so how do I know it's true?" some might say. I can appreciate your desire for accuracy, but wouldn't you agree with 1 John 4:8 that "God is love"? And from Scripture, God's own definition of love is this:

> Love is patient, love is *kind*. It does not envy, it does not boast, it is not proud. It is *not rude*, it is not self-seeking, it is not easily angered, it keeps *no record of wrongs*. Love does not delight in evil but rejoices with the truth. It always *protects*, always *trusts*, always *hopes*, always *perseveres*. Love *never* fails. (1 Cor. 13:4–8)

If God is love, then God is *kind*, not rude. He is also always looking to *trust you* and to *protect you*, and he *never fails you*. In other words, he's in your corner every single time! Although these words may help us believe our God is good to us all the time, the reality is that there are actually *no* words strong enough to capture the goodness of God toward us. God's love for us surpasses knowledge!

In the work of the Son, we see the heart of a Father.

And I pray that you, being rooted and established in love, may have power, together with all the saints, to grasp how *wide* and *long* and *high* and *deep* is the love of Christ, and to know *this love that surpasses knowledge*—that you may be filled to the measure of all the fullness of God. (Eph. 3:17–19)

How is this kind of relentless love made possible? The Father divinely arranged for all his righteous anger and all of his justice to fall on Jesus at the cross. In the work of the Son, we see the heart of a Father who accepts us with no strings attached. His affection toward us is stronger than we can possibly imagine.

DADDY'S NEW WAY

We all want to know the love of God. We may plead and beg to know it. We may look up into the sky, clench our fists, and scream out to God that we want to feel his love. But God's love is experienced *through Jesus*. And the new covenant inaugurated in Jesus's blood is the clearest way God has ever demonstrated his love for us:

But God *demonstrates* his own love for us *in this*: While we were still sinners, Christ died for us. (Rom. 5:8)

See how God demonstrated his love? We will have an incredibly difficult time grasping the love of God without a clear understanding of the new covenant. In fact, the new covenant is the *only* message the church is qualified to share today:

He has made us *competent as ministers of a new covenant*—not of the letter but of the Spirit; for the letter kills, but the Spirit gives life. (2 Cor. 3:6)

The new covenant is where it's at! Our Daddy's new way is about realizing the unlimited forgiveness he gave us. And it's about embracing our intimate union with his Son, Jesus. But it's not just about new covenant doctrine.

We can know the Daddy beyond the doorway.

Doctrine is the doorway. The forgiveness and freedom we have in Christ mean we can know the Daddy beyond the doorway.

In religion, it's popular to hear that we need more: We need more forgiveness. We need more of the Spirit. We need to thirst for more of God. We need to hunger for more of Jesus. Our Daddy's new way is the polar opposite. He's saying we have everything we need:

For in Him all the fullness of Deity dwells in bodily form, and *in Him you have been made complete*, and He is the head over all rule and authority. (Col. 2:9–10 NASB)

His divine power has given us *everything we need for life and godliness* through our knowledge of him who called us by his own glory and goodness. (2 Pet. 1:3)

What does it mean to you to be complete? For me, it means *the search is over*. No more hungering. No more thirsting. No more waiting for more:

> He who comes to me will *never go hungry*, and he who believes in me will *never be thirsty*. (John 6:35)

The sales pitch of religion is that we're lacking; we're dirty; and we're distant. Through more commitments and more dedication, we can get clean and get close to God. So we go from church to church, conference to conference, and movement to movement, looking for something more, something deeper.

Religion says, "Make every effort." God says, "Make every effort to rest in me." Instead of hoping and waiting for more, we're invited to the intimate union with Jesus we've already been given.

We're invited to God, without religion.

ACKNOWLEDGMENTS

First, I want to thank my wife, Katharine, for her incredible support while I was completing this book. Katharine, I love you and cherish all that God has made you to be. I am so honored to be married to you.

I also want to recognize my mother, Leslie Farley, for her love and encouragement to me over the years. She is truly a woman of grace, and I am privileged to have her in my life.

In addition, I am blessed to have the love and support of Doug and Maurita Hayhoe. Thank you for always being in my corner.

I am so grateful to the leadership and members of Ecclesia. Their encouragement gave me a tremendous boost as I completed this book. In particular, I want to thank Rex Kennedy, Steven Bailey, Jordan Polk, and Kim Martin.

A special thank-you goes to Andrea Heinecke at Alive Communications for her insights and help throughout the process. I am also thankful for my friends Lee Higginbotham and Andy Lavery and the support they gave me.

I want to express my appreciation to Rob Jackson at Extra Credit Projects for the design of the book cover. And I want to thank Baker Books for partnering with me in this ministry. In particular, I'd like to acknowledge Robert Hosack, Wendy Wetzel, Bobbi Jo Heyboer, Brooke Nolen, and Paula Gibson.

Finally, I want to thank my Lord and Savior Jesus Christ for the opportunity to express on paper what he has placed in my heart.

Andrew Farley is lead pastor of Ecclesia (ChurchWithout Religion.com) and bestselling author of *The Naked Gospel: The Truth You May Never Hear in Church*. Andrew's writings are quietly reaching untold numbers with the life-changing message of "Jesus plus nothing." Andrew is a tenured professor at Texas Tech University, where he offers courses in linguistics and an honors course in New Testament. He lives on the high plains of West Texas with his wife, Katharine, and their son, Gavin. Find out more about Andrew at AndrewFarley.org, and connect with him on Facebook and Twitter.

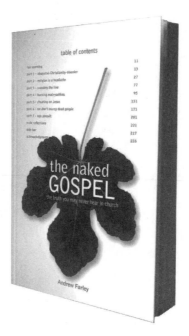

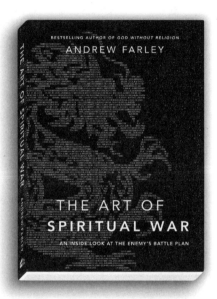

The Hurt & The Healer

Where Glory Meets Our Suffering

Fear. Shame. Loneliness. A broken home. A broken heart. We all hurt, and we all need healing. We just don't know where to find it. Inspired by the #1 Christian single "The Hurt & The Healer" from MercyMe, this book shows how Jesus can take our hearts and breathe them back to life, how "grace is ushered in for good, and all our scars are understood."

Are you ready to discover how Jesus can be the Healer of your hurts?

Available now!

Relax. Revel in the neglected spiritual discipline.

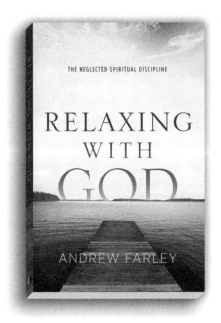

Relaxing with God shares biblical wisdom on the neglected art of resting in Christ. Anyone longing to experience true release from the crushing expectations that the world throws their way will find life and rest in Farley's revolutionary message.

"Very few Christians know what it means to rest in Christ. But as Andrew writes, rest is Jesus's promise to every believer. Are you ready to loosen your grip on all the religious traditions? Are you ready to let go of all the worry and self-effort? If so, I encourage you to read this book carefully. Soak in the truth of God's love and grace. It's time for you to relax with God and enjoy his life to the full."

—BOB CHRISTOPHER, president of Basic Gospel (BasicGospel.net)

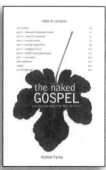